# DON'T CALL ME GRANDMA!

# DON'T CALL ME GRANDMA!

## A Guide for the 21st-Century Grandmother

# ILENE LEVENTHAL

DON'T CALL ME GRANDMA!
A GUIDE FOR THE 21ST-CENTURY GRANDMOTHER

iUniverse books may be ordered through booksellers or by contacting:

iUniverse
1663 Liberty Drive
Bloomington, IN 47403
www.iuniverse.com
1-800-Authors (1-800-288-4677)

Because of the dynamic nature of the Internet, any web addresses or links contained in this book may have changed since publication and may no longer be valid. The views expressed in this work are solely those of the author and do not necessarily reflect the views of the publisher, and the publisher hereby disclaims any responsibility for them.

Any people depicted in stock imagery provided by Thinkstock are models, and such images are being used for illustrative purposes only. Certain stock imagery © Thinkstock.

ISBN: 978-1-4917-8162-3 (hc)

Library of Congress Control Number: 2015918474

Print information available on the last page.

iUniverse rev. date: 11/10/2015

# DEDICATION

To all grandmothers
past, present, and future.

To my adoring husband, Norm,
the love of my life,
for always cheering me on.

To my amazing children, Lisa,
Brian, Shawn, Scott & Bonnie
for their unconditional love and support.

And, of course, to my most precious
and adoring grandchildren,
Jaclyn Rose, Cole Samuel, Camryn
Ava, Isaac Reid, Todd Harrison
and those yet to come …
you all light up my life everyday and have
given me the gift of being your Nana!

# ACKNOWLEDGEMENTS

A very special thanks to my editor,
Jon Hueber
for his patience and guidance.

To my talented sister-in-law, Karen
for creating and sketching the
Grandma on the cover of this book.

My heartfelt gratitude to Lisa,
my loving daughter
for suggesting I write about a subject
near and dear to my heart
GRANDMOTHERHOOD!
and for giving me my extraordinary
first granddaughter, Jaclyn Rose.

# TABLE OF CONTENTS

# PROLOGUE
# THE LITTLE YELLOW BOOK

This little yellow book is going to be your best friend! I was actually going to call it *"The Yellow Pages,"* because this book is designed to guide you in a way that the famous little phonebook used to guide us before technology brought us the internet. However, my dear husband, Norm, the lawyer, said I could not use that name because of something called a trademark. But you can think of it as your personal Yellow Pages when it comes to being a grandmother here in the 21st century.

*DON'T Call Me Grandma!* is primarily written for the "grandma-to be," and could be a cute gift for the occasion to congratulate a new grandma, or for a Mother's Day gift, or even a Grandparents' Day gift (yes, thanks to the greeting card companies, we now have a day in September just for us. It's sometime before Arbor Day and just after National Canned Soup Day. Check your calendars). Grandmas of all ages everywhere can use the information contained within these pages.

*DON'T Call Me Grandma!* is also tailored for parents to understand "Grandma's side of the story" and therefore will also be appropriate to give a new mom. Not to be outdone, there is also value in this book for grandpas and new fathers. In short, this book is for everybody. Don't let the title fool you.

Okay, enough of the hard sell, you're holding the book so you are at least interested in what I have to say. Let's get to the heart of this little yellow guidebook. I am now going to enlighten you. Just because your children are pregnant does not mean that you are. Yes, you've "been there, done that," but they couldn't care less; that was then, this is now. So don't think you have earned the right to be their coach, their mentor, or their resident know-it-all. Save the advice until you are asked for it (and you will be asked), no matter how difficult this will be for you; it will pay off in the long run (maybe!).

You know why pregnant couples cannot wait to be called Mommy or Daddy? It's because they have worked really hard to earn their coveted title. Whether by recreation, planned, or by accident, a new life is on its way. Or, in some cases, science is involved and creating a new life takes meticulous planning, praying, and a little luck. In those instances, they have spent months turning steamy spontaneous sex into a scientific formula. Regardless of how it happens, it happens all for the greater good.

Once they know they are pregnant, phase two begins and they're off, so you had better not put your two cents in while they are heavily into the planning stage. Believe me I know it is difficult, as this is your son or daughter, who you raised yourself (yes, probably with *some* help from your husband). Try to remember, this is their time and you must give the-parents-to-be the space needed to make their own decisions. Of course you should be there to support them, the truth is that you are delegated to the sidelines to observe and to be a resource for them and to answer any questions they may ask. However don't hold your breath, and try not to be upset if those questions don't come during the pregnancy. Trust me, the questions will come later; in some cases much later, but they will come. They have some tough decisions to make which they themselves probably won't agree on until they find common ground; it's tough enough for two people to agree, let alone a third party adding to the confusion. They have to decide on things like: do they want to find out the sex of their unborn child? What should they name their baby? And after all of the important questions are taken care of, then they will get around to what's really important here: what they want this precious child-to-be to call you!

So you may as well sit back and relax until they are ready to share their decisions with you; try very hard to be patient. If you remember, as a grandmother-to-be, nine months of pregnancy is not the easiest thing to experience. Enduring those raging hormones was tough, but even tougher on our husbands and partners once they realized that we no longer had control over our bodies. Sure, there were plenty of wonderful moments during those 36 weeks, but they were quickly forgotten when the "hormone witch" appeared. I am telling you all of the above so that you will be more sensitive to their needs. And by all means wait a while before jumping in with what you experienced during your pregnancy; your kids don't want to hear it.

There is so much that can be said about how you can negotiate *their* pregnancy, all the while keeping the peace and not stressing out yourself. I hope these chapters will help cushion the ride by providing you with some valuable tips. For this book, I have interviewed many grandmothers from our generation (I am in my late sixties); it seems that the toughest thing to remember is that you are no longer in the driver's seat. That is reserved for parents only, and nobody likes a backseat driver. If asked directions, feel free to share your opinion, otherwise, sit back and try to enjoy the ride. You may end up with a sore mouth from biting your tongue, but ultimately, you will reap the benefits. Remember that the driver, no doubt, will take a different route than you took when you were driving. It's okay; it's human nature. Today they have the beltway, the freeway, and the highway, just not your way, because parenting is very different than our way; which to some is now viewed as the wrong way!

For example, disciplining a child in today's world makes no sense to us. If our children sassed us, or didn't listen, there was nothing wrong with giving them a little smack on the tush. Today that would be considered a misdemeanor, punishable by law! So don't say a word when your grandchild is put in a "time out" for the fifth time that day for repeating the same offense an hour later after they finished the first time out. My husband and I find it very amusing when bedtime rolls around and our daughter says to her little ones, "Okay, upstairs in five minutes." And then when five minutes are up the kids ask for "final minute." This usually goes on for another ten minutes. Norm and I look at each other and roll our eyes but never say a word; again, it's not easy from the backseat, but to be in the car on this incredible journey, this is where we have to sit. Luckily, our daughter and her wonderful husband don't get upset with us when we offer advice. They just ignore us, and honestly, it's probably better that way.

Having said all of the above, you do have certain inalienable rights as a grandparent. You know, other than "you have the right to remain silent on the grounds that you will definitely incriminate yourself." It's always best to sit down with your grown children and draw up a "Grandparent's Bill of Rights." We will discuss the Grandparent's Bill of Rights in a later chapter, but it is important to draw one up early in the process. Make it part of the early planning stages and there can be no objections later when those rights are challenged. And they will be challenged.

You've experienced childhood and motherhood; now fasten your seatbelt because you are in for the ride of your life: Grandmother Hood! My purpose in writing this book is to help you get through the bumps you will most likely encounter along the way, and to give advice and guidance as best as I can when those bumps become mountains. Always remember to take a lot of deep breaths. Keep the peace within yourself, as well as learn to exercise some control over how you choose to act as a new grandma. If you can do that, all will work out splendidly and if it doesn't, you can easily take some of the advice offered in this book.

So for now, read on and hopefully you will find some valuable tips and pointers among these chapters. These are just suggestions, a sharing of ideas from one grandma to another, or soon-to-be-grandma. I have said this before, but it truly is the first rule to remember; practice taking deep breaths, try and try again to relax, and if you can do this, you are sure to enjoy the ride, bumps and all.

# CHAPTER 1

# A LIFE ALTERING MOMENT

So, your kids have been trying to conceive. Or maybe it was a complete surprise. One way or another, they are pregnant, but your life has gone on as usual. Your days are still filled with going to work, going to the gym, meeting the girls for lunch, shopping at your favorite stores, volunteering for your favorite charity, and whatever else you do that makes up your typical day. Life is good.

Life has a way of changing quickly, and that change happens when you get that phone call and you hear your ecstatic son or daughter say with joy dripping off their words: "Guess what, Mom? We're pregnant!" The first thought through your head will probably be one of sheer joy (or panic, depending on the circumstances, but for our purposes, this will be a joyous occasion), but then that will be replaced with: "What do you mean *we're* pregnant?" When I was pregnant with my children, I always said, "guess what? *I'M* pregnant!"

I was the one who blew up like a balloon. I was the one with swollen ankles. And I was the one constantly hanging my head over the toilet for the first four months. I don't remember my husband having to get up to pee all night long. I gained so much weight with my first child that my poor husband had to literally lift my legs up in order for me to swing them into the car, all while listening to me bitch and moan about how uncomfortable I was. Even as all of those horrors came rushing back to me, it felt perfectly natural to my pregnant daughter to share the event by saying "we're pregnant!" I guess her husband did have *something* to do with it, so why shouldn't he be pregnant as well. And I'd like to think that I was part of that too. Sure, I wasn't going through it all over again, but my knowledge and my experience could be vital. I could be a member of their team. Maybe I was a "we're" as well!

And that train of thinking leads me to my first point. Rule number one: If you want to be a good grandparent you must learn to keep things to yourself. I know I said this earlier, but it is so worth repeating. At that very moment you hear the words, "we're pregnant," you will most likely be overwhelmed with joy and excitement. That is, until you hear the voice on the other end of the line shout, "you're going to be a Grandma!" And then your world stops. Everything that you held dear; going to work; those trips to the gym, lunch with the girls, shopping, etc., have all come to a screeching halt. You are now a different person, complete with a different title. You are frozen, except for your mouth, which has fallen wide open, but you don't even notice because you have immediately slipped into a state of panic and shock. Your mouth becomes dry and all you hear is *Grand* and *Mother*. Those two words, over and over, as though saying it will age you instantly. The voices in your head begin to shout words like *old, over the hill, old, gray hair, old, granny glasses, old, and one more old for good measure*. When I first heard I was going to be a grandmother, visions of my own Grandma wearing orthopedic shoes, a flowery apron and white hair held up with a net. I saw images of her removing her false teeth to rinse them off every night, and of her support hose that never seemed to stay up over her calves. Scary stuff.

I know you probably hadn't really thought about all of these things prior to hearing the news. Your focus was on hoping that the kids could and would get pregnant, but now faced with the reality that it's happened, a wave of fear crashes over you as you sit there with the phone attached to your head, mouth agape.

Of course you were waiting for this to happen and often thought about how much fun it would be to have a child that you could love and play with, and then give back to mommy and daddy when you were done. It seemed so simple; you would have all of the benefits of having a little adorable baby with none of the hassles or responsibilities that go along with caring for and raising a child. Sorry friends, let me be the first to say that just ain't the way it works. Then it truly hits you like a ton of bricks and you think to yourself, "GRANDMA? Please don't call me GRANDMA!"

CHAPTER 2

# THE GRANDPARENT'S BILL OF RIGHTS

As previously mentioned, it's a good idea for grandparents-to-be to sit down and come up with a set of rules -- rights, actually -- that lay out the groundwork for the role of the grandparent going forward. Here, we call them:

## GRANDPARENT'S BILL OF RIGHTS

1. **We have the right to decide what we want our grandkids to call us.**
2. **We have the right to spoil them because that's what grandparents do.**
3. **We have the right NOT to remain silent if we feel it necessary to bring something to your attention.**
4. **We have the right to JUST SAY NO!**
5. **We have the right to give them their favorite candy and sugared cereal when they sleep over.**

6. We have the right to demand respect from our grandkids and our children.
7. We have the right to give our grandkids gifts for no reason.
8. We have the right to be informed of all medical issues concerning our grandkids.
9. We have the right to take them to McDonalds once in a while.
10. We have the right to cherish and love them forever.

# CHAPTER 3

# WHAT'S IN A NAME?

This part you are going to like. Number one in the Grandparent's Bill of Rights is that you get to pick what you want the little one to call you. If your grown son or daughter tries to make you feel guilty about selecting your own name/title by saying something like, "but we always wanted our children to call you 'Grandma.' It's been a tradition in our family for generations." Simply let them know that you will be a wonderful grandmother (at least you hope to be), the only difference is that you want to be called something that fits you, whether culturally (which we will get to in Chapter 14), or based on your lifestyle, or even based on your family tradition. "Grandma" is bland and passé, especially with so many interesting names to choose from (see the list in appendix A). More than likely, they still haven't even decided on a boys or girls name for the coming bundle of joy, and they have been talking about it since they decided to get pregnant, and in some cases, have probably been talking about it since they first got married.

Now is when you can grab the upper hand. Remind them that you don't really get a choice in the naming of their child, so they should afford you the same courtesy. This actually happened to a friend of mine and she did step up to the plate and was able to flex her right by casually telling her daughter-in-law: "When you decided to have a baby and began to think of names, I suggested Sophie or Perry. You both told me to forget it and that you wanted a more modern name like Raven or Atlanta (at the time all I could think about was the Baltimore football team, or the state of Georgia). I hope you both noticed that I haven't said a word to you since (though I silently prayed for a more normal name that didn't remind me of a sport or a place on the map). Don't you both think that you owe me the same courtesy?"

The title that a grandparent will be called is almost sacred. This is the name for which you will be called, more than likely, until your last days on this earth. And don't be afraid to let your children know that. And if it comes down to it, you can always play the trump card and threaten to withhold certain grand-parental obligations. It's dirty, and a little low, but hey, we are talking about naming rights here. It's important! If it comes to it, don't be afraid to say, "don't mess with me or I will never baby sit for you," and "you probably don't want me angry or spiteful as you're gonna need me!" Okay, maybe that second one is a bit too harsh, but you understand what I'm saying. Again, this is important. Not only to you, but to the unborn child waiting to be held in his or her grandparent's loving arms.

If the conversation gets to this point, a calming period will most certainly bring tensions down a notch. In my friend's case (and yes, she did threaten to withhold babysitting services and did inform them that they were going to need Grandma), her daughter-in-law backed down by saying, "We won't discuss it now. We have nine months to convince you." She said it with a light-hearted chuckle, but she got the message across loud and clear; it was game on!

Offer something on your end as well. Tell the mommy-and-daddy-to-be (or the pregnant couple) that you promise to come up with a name before their baby is born, and they will surely be the first to know what name _you_ decide on. If they are upset, stand your ground! It might just be the one and only thing you have control over once their precious little bundle of joy is born.

Pick a name that makes you feel good. When you say it out loud you will know immediately that it is what you are meant to be called by your precious grandchildren.

As I previously mentioned, I have provided you with a list of name suggestions and I promise they are all names that hip grandmothers, like yourself, have chosen. I did an extensive survey and I am even offering you some names in other languages to give you more options in case you do not want to be called "Grandma."

Before I go on any further I must make it clear to those of you who like being called grandma that I am in no way implying that it reflects an image of being old. Quite the contrary. You may have chosen "Grandma" because of tradition or because you are honoring your grandmother. If this applies to you please don't stop reading (if you haven't already tossed it) my little yellow book. We love and respect that. Honestly, there is no wrong answer here. You will know the right name, whether it is classic and traditional, or hip and savvy. The key issue here is that the choice should always be yours, with one caveat.

There are plenty of grandmothers who decide on a name after their precious grandchild mispronounces their original "name of choice." Grandma just couldn't resist that adorable smile and that tiny little hand reaching for her while repeating that unintelligible name. That jumbled word of sounds and syllables can become your name and it can stick. A perfect example of this comes from my sister, Phyllis. She now answers to *Rag'm*. When her first grandchild was born, Phyllis wanted to be called simply "Grandma." Each time the little darling tried to say the word "Grandma" it came out as Rag'm. Being the loving and easygoing woman Phyllis is, she decided that Rag'm would be her title going forward. She felt very special to have had her first grandchild name her. I think it's pretty safe to say that none of us would have gone with that one (sorry Phyllis!) but for my sister, it works and it is her identity.

After all these years and five grandchildren later, I have never laughed at her name; at least not in front of her. Phyllis must be more self-confident than I am because I would have worked endlessly to change that pronunciation ASAP! But hey, that's what this is all about; going with the name that makes *you* feel good. Some people like chocolate, others vanilla or strawberry; so what if Phyllis chose tutti fruiti? Just remember, whatever the name is, it's all about YOUR choice.

By the way, I am **Nana** to my five beautiful grandchildren. There was never a question in my mind because my mom was Nana to my children. I clearly remember her saying that she never wanted to be called grandma because she felt so young, and to her "Grandma" was for someone with white hair. Now that she is gone, every time my grandchildren call me Nana I think of my mom, which warms my heart. I do wish that I had asked her why she chose Nana because in 1969 (when my first child was born) "Nana" was not a common choice. The only Nana I knew was the dog in Walt Disney's *Peter Pan*. But I did love that Nana, too.

After extensive research on alternative names for "Grandma," it seems that most grandmothers have had a name in mind even before their grandchild was ever born. And in many cases, once their little one learned to make sounds and happened to repeat the same sound whenever she went to visit, that is the name that stuck, as in the story of my sister, Phyllis.

Why? Because she was so excited that the little one identified her by name that she was suckered in. Who wouldn't be?

If you are still on the fence on what to be called, I've found in interviewing grandmas worldwide that you have a better chance of selecting a two syllable name, like Mimi, Gigi, or Nana simply because they are easier to pronounce. On the other hand, if you select a longer, more complicated name, you can continue to correct that little pumpkin until he/she finally gets it. You may have to wait a few years, but remember: if it's important to you, the wait will be worth it. Once again, the choice is ultimately yours!

# CHAPTER 4

# I REMEMBER GRANDMA

I was lucky enough to grow up with two grandmothers. I had a Grandma Fannie and a Grandma Rose. When I think about them I get such a warm and fuzzy feeling deep inside. The images that I conjure up when they come to mind are of gray hair tucked neatly inside gray hairnets, ruffled aprons tied across their waist, and thick soled, and very plain orthopedic shoes. Both of my grandmothers wore little pearl earrings and each had a lovely antique wedding ring.

Whenever my parents took us all out to dinner, a beautiful strand of pearls would appear on my Grandma Fannie's neck. She lived with us from the time I was born until she became very ill at the young age of sixty-five. Of course, she looked eighty-five compared to a 65-year old woman today. I am now 69 years old and still feel like I am in my thirties (the trick is not to look in a magnified mirror!) We all have to grow old, but where is it written that we have to act it, or for that matter, look it?

When my thoughts turn to Grandma Fannie I can still see her standing at the front door waiting to greet me each afternoon with a big hug after my very long walk home (I had to walk to and from school, both ways, up hill, in snow and rain; sound familiar?). It was as though my walking through that door was the highlight of her day; actually, as I reminisce, I think it might have been. Her smile reminded me of that yellow happy face from Wal-Mart bouncing around the store reducing prices!

The only time Grandma Fannie's apron came off was when we went out as a family, or on the few occasions when she took me downtown to see a movie. I do not think any of my friends' grandmother's knew how to drive, and neither did mine. We would walk to the bus stop and after a short ride, transfer to a streetcar. In cooler weather (and in my memories, it was always cool, or cold), she always wore her long, gray wool coat, the same color gloves, and a little Jackie-Kennedy-style hat with a short veil that stopped at her forehead. And of course, she carried the same pocketbook every time. It was a bit worn, but she loved it nevertheless, holding on to it so tightly as though it had been full of precious jewels.

My mom was forever trying to take my grandma shopping to buy her a new dress or purse. Grandma Fannie consistently refused, saying the same thing each time mom asked, "How many dresses can I wear at one time? What I have is all I need."

That was my grandmother's mindset.

Whenever my mom bought my sisters or me a new dress, Grandma Fannie always gave her a hard time. It was, however, understandable; she lived through the depression and, unfortunately, never was able to shed that mentality.

If you find me a grandma in this day and age that only owns two dresses, one pair of shoes and one purse, then I will give you a million dollars (just a figure of speech to get my point across. My lawyer husband was adamant that I explain that). My reason for sharing this with you is that I am sure you had a grandmother somewhat like mine. Maybe not a grandmother exactly as I have described, but someone who, in your memories, is a timeless icon to a day long since passed.

I know I have told you a lot about my Grandma Fannie because she lived with us, so naturally I was very close to her. My other grandmother, Grandma Rose, was also a big part of my life when I was growing up. I remember going to her house every Friday night with my parents and sisters. I loved going there and looked forward to Friday knowing that we would be going to Grandma Rose's house for a delicious dinner and a fun-filled evening. After dinner we would eat her famous chocolate pudding. It was because of Grandma Rose that I became addicted to it. I thought it was yummy but as I got older I wasn't too thrilled with the film of chocolate over the pudding, which I referred to as "chocolate pudding skin." My sisters and I practiced skits and songs and dances all week so we could perform for everyone. Grandma Rose rolled back the area rug to give us more room to dance and jump around. I can still remember her clapping her hands while we sang, danced or acted silly. She had the biggest grin on her face. You would have thought she was watching a Broadway performance. Looking back, we were pretty bad, but according to Grandma Rose, we were extremely talented.

Grandma Rose never took me anywhere and barely got out herself. I only saw her on Friday nights, and on Sundays when my Dad would pick her up and bring her to our house. She had a sister who was our great aunt. Grandma Rose always argued with her and never really got along with her. It all started when Grandma Rose came to the United States from Poland; she was only about seven or eight-years-old. When she arrived at Ellis Island, she chose the name Rose. Her sister came a few years later and also chose the name Rose. So she was my Great Aunt Rose. The funny thing is that my Mom's name was also Rose, but she was named that by Grandma Fannie when she was born. Grandma Rose didn't know my Mom until she started dating my Dad, so she thought it was funny that they had the same name. However, Great Aunt Rose committed the cardinal sin by picking the same name as her sister and was very aware of it, but liked the name so she selected it anyway. Grandma Rose never forgave her for that. She said that her sister was jealous of her and "stole my name to be mean."

I thought it was very sad that they never got along because Grandma Rose refused to forgive Great Aunt Rose. My sisters and I were always close and I truly thought it was that way in all families, or at least it should have been. Two Roses are one Rose too many, I suppose.

Time marches on so fast, that even newly minted grandparents will be considered "ancient" by the time their grandchildren reach adulthood. Even grandparents who today were on the forefront of the internet age, who were the first to send texts via a phone, and watch 1,000 channels on the television, they too will be outdated well before their time. The secret to overcoming this is to think and feel young, no matter what. Grandchildren should never age you. They are, in fact, largely responsible for keeping us young. I'll get more in depth with this in the next chapter.

# CHAPTER 5

# FOREVER YOUNG

After you get past the name issue, the weight of the situation hits you again. No matter what name you choose, you will still be a grandmother. A mother to a mother; a second-generation mother; a GRAND mother! This will probably freak you out if you let it. I promise you that you will not age quicker because you suddenly become a grandmother. If you refuse to let your self-image change, then the way others view you will not change. It's all in the mind. I know it's such a cliché to say, "you're only as old as you feel," but it's true. I prefer to say, "you're only as young as you feel and act." This is also so very true, and I am sure most of you already know this. I have friends and sisters who are so "young at heart" that they can outlast their grandchildren in the high-energy department.

As a matter of fact, it's a pretty neat feeling when you take your little grandchild out shopping, or for an ice cream, or to the park and people think you are the mother. It's a fantastic boost to your ego! But remember; in order for this to happen be sure to wear a pair of those tight jeans with a "cool" print t-shirt that all the kids are wearing today.

I am the Modern Day Grandma. I'm young at heart, full of a zest for life and my closet is still full of heels, boots, work-out shoes, comfortable "around the house" shoes, and flip flops (I am sure I missed a few categories). Dress young and you'll feel young has always been my motto. When playing tennis, golf, or any outdoor sport there is more "freedom of dress." There are not many different outfits for these sports; for example, most tennis outfits consist of short skirts so you can move around the courts more easily. When playing tennis we get to dress like everyone else, no matter what their age is. So the 16-year-old girl in the next court could possibly have on the same tennis outfit that you are wearing, which is quite acceptable. But the real trick is to dress young but not look like you are trying to. In other words, the mini-skirts, midriff tops, tight jeans with the popular holes in them are definitely not for us. I used to wear skirts and dresses a few inches above my knees but now I feel like that would put me in the "Oh no, too ridiculous" category. So now, before I buy anything I look in the mirror and say to myself, "Remember, you are now in your late sixties, so does this outfit work?" I tend to answer myself with the right response and "when in doubt, leave it out" always plays a big part in what I buy. However, on the other hand, leggings with the right top (one which covers my derriere) and high boots is a favorite winter look of mine and perfectly acceptable. I may ask my daughter, Lisa, who is 46, if she likes the outfit. We do have different tastes but she will tell me if it's "too young" of a look for me.

There are so many choices for us at our age; dressing young is not only acceptable but encouraged. Look through magazines like *Vogue*, not the ones that cater to young adults. Also, pay attention to what some of the more mature women on the TV talk shows are wearing. I used to wear high heels, which made me feel sexy. Now the style is four-inch and higher. Don't go to the maximum; try to keep the heels to a two-inch height. I am now suffering from foot pains so I couldn't wear the higher heels if I wanted to. That's why I like to wear boots but this only works in the winter. But summertime styles do consist of many great looking flats or very low heels with an open toe. Here's another thing I do to feel young. I love polishing my nails and toenails with the latest colors. I feel good about sporting orange or deep blue polish. My granddaughters have fun picking out colors for me and then I polish their nails as well.

Accessories play an important role in looking young. Remember, you can have fun with costume jewelry, which can also make you feel good. I have a watch that has a metal band with many colors; it is fun and I can't believe how many compliments I get from all ages. The important thing to remember is how you dress; accessorizing is much more forgiving, so feel good about how you are dressing and have fun picking out your purse, jewelry, etc. You know the saying, "clothes make the man" but it should be "clothes and personality make the woman." If you feel good about how you look then your inner-self shines through with a glow of self-confidence and therefore, happiness.

When you try to look the part, you will succeed! I hope by now that you realize that age is definitely a mind game. The key here is to not feel old. There, I said it. And yes, it is that simple. Along with dressing young, there are other things that you can do. The music you listen to, the TV and movies that you watch, the books you read, this one notwithstanding. These are all areas where you can change how you feel, and how you relate to the younger generations, and you can actually keep yourself forever young.

If you have a daughter, has anyone ever come up and said, "I thought you were sisters?" How did that make you feel? It's happened to me and let me tell you, it's almost as good as winning the lottery!

Let's face it, the older (sorry, wrong choice of words) we get the more our ego needs stroking, particularly once you pass age 50. And hey, there's nothing wrong with reaching for that Clairol bottle to chase those grey hairs away. Looking young helps to make you feel young, and as we've already established, feeling young is the key to being a true new age grandma. So, science and chemistry can help you retain that youthful look. It's out there for a reason; don't be afraid to use it. There is absolutely nothing wrong with doing so. You should do whatever it takes to keep that level of energy high.

Personally, I feel grandchildren truly energize you. They have a boundless form of love and energy that acts as the sun to a budding flower, powering enough life-giving light to brighten the darkest day and to make even the oldest person feel young. That's why I put it in this book.

It is very strange, I admit, but I believe this with all of my heart. There have been times where I might have been feeling totally exhausted after a long day at work, or fun times out with the girls, or even shopping, and in much need of more sleep, but when my grandchildren sleep over I can't wait to wake up and start the day with them. I like to make them fun breakfasts, like decorating a pancake to make it look like a happy face, or giving them a cookie with their eggs, rather than a piece of plain old toast. They always think this is the best thing ever and have told me that their mommy would never give them a cookie at breakfast. Mission accomplished! However, I must mention that my daughter knows that I do this, and is fine with whatever I want to do (I am lucky that way). I'm not condoning spoiling your grandchildren with sweet treats and poor nutritional choices. I do explain to my grandchildren that I would never have given their mom a cookie for breakfast, and that makes it so much more special in their eyes. That's why it's so great to be a Nana, and my grandchildren definitely agree.

After breakfast I am ready to do whatever my grandchildren want to do; no naps needed today, as my adrenalin (and the sugar rush from the cookie, of course I have one as well) keeps me running. It's as though my energy tank gets filled to the brim by those little munchkins' energy. It is them that keeps me young, that keeps me aware, and that fills me with the joy of being a special part of their lives. Their energy is boundless. That's what you call filling up your tank with love.

Let's take a moment to think back to our childhood, it was a different world! We were very independent. I remember when I was only 11-years-old my mom let me take the bus downtown to see a movie with my best friend Lorraine. We went to dances and parties with boys and never worried about a thing. When my mom was young, her mother never let her go anywhere alone. I do believe that my grandmother's generation was much stricter and definitely more controlling.

Feeling independent is a gift that one receives when allowed to do things on your own. Because my mom didn't want to stifle me like her mom did to her, she went out of her way to let me know that she trusted me. Trust is a big issue and if you are given the gift of trust, I think that makes one trustworthy. How a child is treated growing up has a lasting influence on the type of young adult that child will become. Don't misunderstand me; there were still plenty of rules in our house, some I didn't like and some I didn't follow. However, the consequence of breaking a rule was pretty stiff so I decided it wasn't worth it to ignore the rules I didn't think were fair. In any event, the fact that I could go downtown with a friend to shop or see a movie was very liberating. I am sure that those experiences stayed with me and therefore, the independent Nana I am today is a reflection of those years.

Even if you never experienced this as a child, today's media encourages independence. Our society does not look at us as "over the hill" unless, of course, you act that way.

We can never have too many purses and if you are like me, a closet full of clothes that fit to show off what needs showing off. After all, we have to splurge once in a while; I could never totally give up doughnuts, sweets, or my personal favorite, coconut cake. When I was a young mom I would fit into my smaller size for weekend plans and when Monday rolled around I had eaten so much that I could only fit into the larger size in my closet. So, every Monday it was back to Weight Watchers, Jenny Craig, or the South Beach Diet and going to the gym to work out. Yes, I admit I am a food-a-holic, but it worked for me. Weekday workouts appeased my conscience so with every mile on my treadmill I was already planning on what I wanted to eat Friday night. I hope you were not like me because now that I am in my sixties, it isn't that easy to lose those weekend pounds! No matter what your regiment was, we are definitely not the "grandmothers of yesteryear." And as I mentioned earlier, we got a real buzz when we introduced our daughter and the response was, "you're kidding, you look more like sisters!" I can guarantee that no one ever mistook my mom and my grandmother for sisters. Get my drift?

Meme (Francine), Mimi (Ellen)
and Nana – that's me!
Modern Grandmas Celebrating Halloween in Style

# CHAPTER 6

# FROM THE MOUTHS OF BABES, OR, "GRAMMA, WHY DO YOU HAVE TWO CHINS?"

Do you allow your grandchildren to insult you with the truth? Okay there is no way around this, as children don't use filters. This is a known fact, and instead of ignoring it, or laughing it away, it is up to us, as grandmothers, to loosen up on our bruised egos and to take the bull by the horns and use this to *their* advantage. Just because they're cute, cuddly and totally honest, doesn't mean that you have to grin and bear their insults! There is nothing wrong with teaching your grandchild or grandchildren that even honest observations, and questions like "why is hair growing out of your nose?" can sting, and then explain why. This is a good learning opportunity that will forever help your grandchild in social settings. Laughing when the little one makes fun of your double chins, or when they say publicly after a day walking around the zoo that you smell like stinky feet only reinforces the behavior and can lead to problems down the line. Not curbing this behavior now could put your precious grandchild or grandchildren in a situation where they tell the school bully that he's fat, or much worse.

How you react to this question depends on the kid's age. Don't make them feel badly for hurting your feelings and no pouting, please. I would bet that the child's protective parents would not explain why he/she should not say, "Grandma, you are really fat." Instead, they would just laugh and turn to grandma and say, "Oh, he/she doesn't mean it. It's cute, don't you think?"

When this happened to me I just reminded my daughter about a time when mean comments hurt her. I sat her down and explained to her what she thought when someone said things about her when she was little. This conversation actually happened when my daughter tried to laugh off what was said by calling it "cute":

> *"You think that's cute? Cute like when you were six-years-old, and you came home crying your eyes out because Georgie from next door called you chubby. I don't think you would have liked it if I hadn't told you that he was just being mean because you are so cute and he is the chubby buddy.*

*It made you laugh, and next time you saw Georgie you told him that he said a mean thing to you and demanded he take it back or you would never play with him again. Guess what, he listened because he liked playing with you."*

Address the situation and don't just laugh it off. This is what we call "teaching our children or grandchildren" and it is our responsibility as adults to do so. The grandma can't because she is just the grandma and not the parent here. Oh yeah, just watch me. But not when parents are around. Give your grandchild some credit in the "that's not what we say" department. The kid will get it.

Should you stoop to his/her level and throw insults right back to teach them a lesson? Though it may be tempting at the time, this is a definite no-no. Control your childish instincts. When they say something mean, don't say something back like: "Oh, yeah, well your ears stick out like Dumbo, but do you hear me asking you why?"

Your thoughts are your own so say it in your head and smile. Then answer from the heart in the way that your grandchild will understand and not be sad that your feelings were hurt. Can a grandmother teach her grandchildren right from wrong? Of course. But be careful, as this is a slippery slope. The answer is different in every case.

I am fortunate in that my children expect me to discipline their children when they are with me.

Though I may be a pushover most of the time, I am not afraid to put my foot down. My grandchildren may not like it and will sometimes get angry with me. Not to worry, they will always love you so don't be afraid to lovingly criticize their actions when warranted. Remember to pick your battles; after all, you are not the one who is really responsible for raising them. Thank goodness for that!

# CHAPTER 7

# PARENTHOOD TO GRANDPARENTHOOD

Things were so different back in the 1960s. I got married at 21, had my first child at 23, my second child at 25, and miscarried at 27 with what would have been our third child. I was 31 when I finally had our third child, though in those days it was considered risky to have a child past the age of 30. Most of my friends had all of their children before they turned 30. I must admit that I started noticing wrinkles and grey hairs when I hit that third decade on this earth. I didn't truly appreciate how young I was. Now when I look at photos from back then I am always surprised at how good I looked. I just wish I knew it then.

But I can honestly say that at this point in my life I am much more accepting of my age because on the inside I still feel like a kid. My grandchildren bring out the "silly" in me and each time they laugh because of something I have said or done to make them laugh, I feel so young at heart.

It is much more complicated to be parents today; nothing is as carefree as it was when my children were growing up. It saddens me that my grandchildren have lost the freedom that my children had. For example, my children would play outside unsupervised and sometimes would ride their bikes around the neighborhood until dusk when I would call them in for dinner. They never worried about being snatched up by some bad person, though we did teach our children never to talk to strangers and to never get in a car with a stranger.

That was about the only warning we had to teach them. We felt quite confident that we lived in a safe neighborhood. I felt very comfortable dropping my daughter off at the mall with a friend to spend the day. Birthday parties were in our homes, ice cream, cake, and games were enjoyed by all and sex education was something discussed in high school because there was no need to discuss it *until* then.

The good news is that our grandchildren only know the life they live today; supervised play even on the front lawn is a given. Between their many after school activities (including weekends) their computers, iPads, iPhones, etc., there doesn't seem to be as much family time. We never allowed our children to have TVs in their rooms and I am very happy that my grandchildren don't have them in their rooms either. At least they all watch TV together and for the most part, try to sit down to dinner as a family.

If you take a survey today you will find that most children are involved in at least three "out of school" activities. Aside from so many different sports, dance, music, recitals, games, there is Tae Kwando, Karate, gymnastics and so much more.

My daughter, Lisa and her friend Ilene started a website called **Activityrocket.com**. It's a one-stop shop for parents and even grandparents who are looking for the right activity for their child/grandchild. There are more activities for kids today than you can imagine. I am mentioning this as an example of why kids today are so busy. There are so many choices out there, which is why Activity Rocket is doing so well. Every activity that will appeal to kids today is listed on this site. Also, school starts so much earlier now (I remember going from 9 a.m. to 3 p.m.), and homework, as always, is still a priority; I don't know how they do it.

They, and their parents, are in constant motion; I think it is important for a grandmother to be involved as much as possible and to offer helping with carpools. Actually, this may be the only way you get to see them because "being with Grandma" (or in my case, Nana) does not show up on the calendar hanging on the refrigerator. It is almost impossible to attend each grandchild's games, recitals, plays, etc., so be sure you give your time equally; you may not think they care but I promise you, they do.

Most of my friends understand the unwritten law: "grandchildren come first," and are devoted grandmothers. If we have plans to do something and we get a call that we are needed to take or pick up our grandchild, we will rearrange our schedule to make ourselves available.

For example, I had plans to have lunch with a friend and to see an exhibit at the art gallery that we had wanted to see. The day before I was supposed to go, my granddaughter called me, and in that sweet little voice of hers, asked me a question that halted all other plans.

"Hi Nana. Tomorrow I don't have school because of a teacher's meeting. Will you pick me up and take me with you? Maybe we could see a movie together."

That did it; I was putty in her hands.

"Of course," I heard myself say, "I don't have any plans and would love to spend the day with you."

The great thing about having wonderful friends that are also grandmothers is that we totally understand if one of us cancels at the last minute because of our grandchildren; it's part of the unwritten grandparent law.

*Thou shalt always put our grandchildren first.*

When my children were very young, my mom was a tremendous help; she never said no when I asked her to babysit. However, from the very beginning, she told me that she was always available to babysit, but that I had to bring my children to her house. My husband and I thought it was a fair exchange.

I have adopted the same rule, although I am a bit more flexible in that department, but the choice is mine. You can choose to be a part-time or full-time grandparent as well as deciding if you want to be a good grandmother-in-law or a grandmother-outlaw. Making the positive choice will give you more joy in the long run.

Don't be surprised if at first you don't feel totally attached to your new grandchild. I have been told that many new grandmas feel guilty because they don't really want to visit the little baby every day. That changes drastically once he/she becomes a toddler or begins to recognize you.

My advice is to dutifully visit your children at least once a week so you can "ooh and aah" over that little baby. New parents are very sensitive and expect you to be in awe of their little one because they are, and can't imagine that you wouldn't feel the same way.

# CHAPTER 8

# SHAKING THE "GRANNY IMAGE"

First of all, discard the grandma image in your head, with the flower-print apron and the blue hair and wide-rimmed glasses that frame her aged face with the tray of fresh-baked cookies in her hands; you have full control over it. You know the saying, "What you see is what you get"? Never forget how true this statement is, so go for the visuals. Don't think this is Mission Impossible, because it is not.

There are ways that do not require much of a change on your part. Go through your daily routine and think about what you can do differently to keep you fit, both mentally and physically and I'm not just talking about working out. I sat down and made a list, though it was very intimidating at first. But once I put a few things in writing, it was a breeze.

Here is what I came up with:

- Stop trying to find a parking spot as close to the entrance as possible. A little walk is good for everybody, regardless of age.
- Do short power walks every day. Put those earphones on and listen to your kind of music (whatever music you like. For me, it's Donna Summer, Little Richard, etc. Something upbeat that makes me want to move) that puts a bit of energy in your step.
- If you are a tennis player ask your husband to play singles with you every weekend. If tennis isn't your thing, golf is an excellent, low impact activity. If you crave more, basketball, or just shooting a ball through a hoop (I wasn't suggesting playing a full-court game with the teens down at the park) is a good way to stay active. There are even slow-pitch softball leagues. Playing sports doesn't end when you become a grandparent.
- Sign up for either a Zumba or pole dancing class; both are fun but challenging. If that's too much, try just yoga or assorted water aerobics classes.
- Load your groceries into your car yourself; then when you get home, instead of asking your husband to unload your car, **you** do it yourself. Every little bit of exercise helps to get the heart pumping.

When you turn fifty or sixty no one expects you to have the same energy level that you had in your twenties. People say slowing down at your age is normal. That is truly a crock of #@*#! It is a huge misconception and the fact is that it just ain't so! Here's a perfect example: my sister Arlene (we call her Arlie) is in her seventies and she has more energy than that energizer bunny that just keeps on going. She plays tennis with 30- and 40-year-old women and can outlast them all. Needless to say, they think she is the bionic woman. But the truth behind her constant high energy is two-fold. First of all, she has such an upbeat personality and is so much fun to be with. And second of all, she has been exercising for as long as I can remember, which is when exercising was the new thing, according to Jane Fonda. I even bought her tapes and listened to her instructions to "do it until it burns," which she later discovered that this philosophy was causing injuries.

Thanks Jane; I think my first back surgery was because I listened to her say "Burn Baby Burn."

Getting back to Arlie, I asked her to write a paragraph or two about her exercise choices and why she thinks she can out run her grandchildren.

*"Keeping active was an important part of my life from the time I was a little girl. I swam, I sailed on our family catamaran, played baseball, and did*

a million after school activities and usually had to walk to and from the bus to get to where I was going. I guess my mom was my inspiration because she used to walk up and down Connecticut Avenue and her friends would see her and stop and ask if she needed a ride. In my twenties I developed a love for aerobics whether it was jazzercise, step class, spin class (biking), or just plain low impact aerobics. Sometimes it's tough while you are doing it but when you finish you feel great. My thirties brought tennis into my life and I love it. Singles matches have now turned into doubles, but you can get a darn good work out from good doubles. Playing with most of my grandchildren is the best. Of course the boys are much better than I am now, and it's hard to keep up with them. But it's the best. Tired is not a word I think I ever heard growing up.

I have been blessed with eight active, beautiful, happy grandchildren who range in age from twelve to twenty-two. It has been an incredible journey spending quality time with each one and watching them grow. From driving them to nursery school and picking them up, art class, Gymboree, bowling, making cookies, traveling, shopping, dressing up and going trick or treating, it has been a wonderful ride. And of course we didn't want to miss an athletic event, which ran the gamut from roller blading to volleyball, basketball, soccer, and football."

*Jeremy, Alexis, Kayla, Jack, Nicole, Danny,*
*Grammy (Arlie), Ethan, Kade*

I think the secret to keeping your energy going as you age is to have a positive attitude and always see the glass as "half full" and if you are happy and enthusiastic that gets transmitted to others, especially kids, because they are so perceptive.

I decided to survey about 30 grandmas to see what different activities they enjoy and at the same time build up their energy so when they are with their grandchildren they won't fall apart on the tennis court like I eventually did. A great piece of advice was that in order to stay on track ask a friend or two to join you. You will motivate each other to keep going. You can even treat yourselves to a nice lunch afterwards.

And remember, taking that first step is always the hardest so pick something that you will look forward to doing; grandpa may just want to tango or salsa with you!

- Aerobics Class
- Hiking
- Latin Dance Lessons
- Jazzercise Class
- Horseback Trail Riding
- Nature Walks
- Walking Along The Beach
- Golf
- Line Dancing
- Tennis
- Table Tennis
- Zumba Class
- Swimming
- Water Aerobics
- Bollywood Dance Class
- Brisk Walks
- Join a Bowling Team
- Hiking
- Biking
- Gardening
- Tango Lessons
- Salsa Lessons
- Walking your dog for 45 minutes daily
- Tai Chi
- Nature Walks
- Ballroom Dancing
- Belly Dancing
- Pole Dancing Exercise Classes
- Square Dancing
- Skating/Roller Blading
- Ice Skating
- Step Class

These are only suggestions; you should take the time to make up your own list that you feel is doable. Find unique ways to stay active and you will feel younger. After a while, you will find yourself craving more activity. Then sound the alarm, Grandma is ready to do a ten-mile Tri-Grandma-Athalon! Okay, maybe a five-mile, but you get my point. Am I willing to train for the Tri-Grandma-Athalon? You bet your sweet bottom dollar I am.

Why?

Because I was truly shocked and dismayed when my eight-year-old granddaughter ran me ragged on the tennis court. I thought it would be a piece of cake and that she would beg me to quit after a few sets. But no, instead she made me feel like a tired worn out shoe. She won the first set hands down but I had to tell her I let her win to save face; how pathetic is that? By the second set, my face was beet red and I tried to hide the fact that I could barely catch my breath. I should have known she was too smart for me and she quickly figured it out. Five minutes into the second set she stopped and said, "Nana, let's stop. Don't worry; I didn't think at your age you could play this long. Maybe from now on we should only play doubles."

BUSTED by an eight-year-old!

I tried to hide the fact that I thought I was either having a heart attack or a back spasm. I just smiled and hugged my little showoff. Then I realized that *SHE* was holding *ME* up. That's when I decided to take the gloves off.

When I got home I sat down and looked in the mirror; I made myself stare into the damn thing. I was not about to pull a Snow White and say, "Mirror, mirror on the wall ..." (you know the rest). Then I decided I looked pretty good for my age; probably because my eyesight isn't what it used to be. What a blessing in disguise it is to be half-blind without my glasses or contacts.

"Okay," I said to myself, "I just have to up my game in the stamina department." I always thought I was pretty active. I played doubles with the girls a few times a week; okay, so we take a lot of water breaks and so what if we stop to discuss the latest happenings among our friends. I also go to a stretch/ Yoga class once a week, even though most of the time the music puts me to sleep. I always thought I was getting a lot of exercise when in fact, I was barely moving enough to work up a sweat. It was definitely time to put a plan in motion. Was I motivated enough? Are you kidding? The next time we hit the courts I was going to beat the pants off of that little rascal.

I would show her that her Nana wasn't so old after all. Okay, so I was acting immature about the whole thing, but it did get me to hunker down and make my New Year's Resolutions in May.

This is when I made up the list.

Another important point if you don't want your grandkids to think you are old, even though you are not; I listen to my granddaughter when she tells me what's "cool" to wear. I have things to put on when I am with her and then there are my "normal comfortable" clothes when I am not with my grandchildren that are more suitable for a woman in her sixties.

I listen to their favorite music and pretend to love it even though it makes no sense to me. It floors me that they all (even my four-year-old grandson) know every word to so many songs. I once tried to memorize the words to one of Lady Gaga's songs so I could keep the myth of my coolness in my grandkids eyes alive. But how was I supposed to remember the words to a modern pop song if I can't even remember where I put my car keys?

Aging is a bitch but as long as you try to keep up and understand their lingo, you can probably clear the limbo stick, no matter how low their tiny little arms set it.

So, I am now an official "Peter Pan Nana," because, as Ms. Gaga sings: "Listen to me when I say: I'm on the right track, baby I was born this way."

I have stopped taking naps longer than Todd, my two-year-old grandson. I made the decision to be more active. Not only for my sake, but for the sake of my grandkids. I discovered a wonderful drink that has all the electrolytes and other good stuff to keeps me hydrated and energetic: Coconut Water. Goodbye, diet sodas, and goodbye, Gatorade, I never liked you anyway (not true but if it becomes my mantra I will have more energy). I can't tell you how to live, or what you need to say when you consult the mirror on the wall, but you're reading my book so at the very least, you are open to new ideas.

Get hip, girls! Learn to think like a kid and remember that you were there once upon a time. If you are shaking your head and have decided to be the kind of grandmother that won't allow unwanted interruptions from your grandkids, doesn't care that you can't actively keep up with them, and could care less what anyone thinks, then you have not earned the right to be jealous when your grandchildren make it clear that they prefer to hang out with their friends or worse, their *OTHER* grandmother.

Maybe she has worked hard to be a "modern grandma" who is very involved with her grandchildren and tries to help out with carpools, etc. Maybe she goes for walks every day and tries to remain active and hip so she can remain relevant in their eyes. Maybe she read this book first and is well on her way to becoming the 21st century grandmother! As always, the choice is yours, as it is your life. I can only make suggestions and point you in the right direction. What you do when you aren't reading this book is entirely up to you.

# CHAPTER 9

# THE SWEET, SLIPPERY SLOPE OF GRANDMOTHERHOOD

Feelings run deep in the emotion department. You may have a son/daughter who feels, as parents, they are doing you a favor by letting their little one sleep over. It is difficult for them to entrust their precious baby to anyone. Don't take it personally; when their first child is born they want to do everything by the book. They are like deer caught in headlights; frozen in fear of making a wrong choice. Many moms from my generation touted Dr. Spock and followed his advice to the letter, at least for their first child. If you were one of those moms and someone else (your mom or a friend) suggested something that was contrary to what Doc Spock had to say, what was your response? That's what I thought. So you can understand why they will panic if you try to alter their much thought-out schedule they hand you along with their little one. The new parents will go over the schedule a thousand times with you before they actually leave your home. They don't understand, nor do they care that you raised him/her and never dropped him/her nor did you ever leave them alone in a bathtub to drown. Remember they are new to "The Parenting Game" so you have to cut them some slack. Just keep nodding your head but try not to nod off. Give the new mom some time to feel comfortable in her new role and praise her "mommy skills."

She will eventually come around once she feels she has your respect and hopefully will listen to some minor suggestions. Test the waters and tread lightly, meaning one suggestion at a time. But for now don't try to change anything they have written; you may think your children could never make it without you taking their little angel off their hands for a night or two. Think again, my friend. Would a mother lion allow her cub to be in the hands of another unfit lioness? I have seen this happen when a friend told her daughter-in-law that she didn't follow the schedule to the letter, bragging that Grandma's way was far better. To Grandma's dismay, that was the last time that little baby was dropped off for a sleepover until she was a toddler. But don't panic because once the parents leave there's nothing wrong with using your skills to alter the schedule a bit; just keep it to yourself. I am talking about the five-page schedule/list of rules that gives you minute-to-minute instructions. Don't laugh; this has happened to many grandmothers.

However, if the schedule is reasonable it is best to follow it. No need to ruffle feathers, but use your best judgment. The fact that *your* children just dropped off *their* child/children is proof that you know what you're doing.

Okay, this may sound terrible, but until your grandchild can talk, as I mentioned a moment ago, it is more than fine to alter the schedule/rules their parents have given you. But once that little one can talk, watch out; as soon as mom walks in your door the kid will blurt out, "Guess what mom, Nana took me to the candy store at the mall and let me eat whatever I wanted to, but don't tell because it is our secret!"

Busted again.

They can't be trusted and they will tell on you so beware; there is no code of silence between a child and his/her mom. Now you are really in trouble because you have broken the cardinal sin by allowing your grandchild to ingest all that sugar, or worse. It may take a while before you regain mom's trust.

You will most likely find that most moms today are extremely health conscious, and in my opinion, sometimes to a fault. If you don't shop at Whole Foods or Fresh Fields and learn to read labels you are hampering the growth and wellbeing of their child.

Well to that I say bull*@*#! We grandmothers also want the best for our grandchildren, but we see nothing wrong with giving them what they want once in a while. But having said that, don't get upset and try to change their mind, I've found from experience that it just won't work. They are from a different generation, almost from another world. We would feed our kids anything and not think twice about what foods were processed, etc. Remember, back then there were no labels of ingredients on boxes, jars, or cans. I would feed my toddlers hot dogs, pieces of American cheese, or slices of salami. So you may say to your daughter/son, "I fed you whatever you wanted and you turned out okay."

Well, the truth is that the environment has become quite toxic; we all know that in recent years farmers have begun feeding their animals hormones to fatten them up, not to mention the pesticides that are tainting our fruits and vegetables. All of this and more is exactly why "organic" is the new buzzword.

If we knew the facts we would cringe at what goes into some of the foods we eat. So there are definitely legitimate concerns that we need to be aware of and respect. I am very lucky because my daughter allows me to take my grandchildren to a fast food restaurant once in a while. She feels that when her children are with their Nana (that's me) it is a special time and therefore allows me to take them pretty much wherever they want to go.

A trip to McDonalds is a special treat because only Nana would take them there. And this is a generational thing. I think my daughter was so lenient because I let my mom (her Nana) feed her whatever she wanted when they were together. Only a grandma can spoil a child because we don't have them that often.

After the "newness" of being a Nana wore off I did become more tuned in to giving my grandchildren more healthy choices. My youngest granddaughter loves sweets and can never get enough. I mean she's a real choc-o-holic! I don't want to encourage this so now I will give her one cookie rather than three. She sometimes begs for more but I don't give in; and guess what, she still loves me and loves to be with me. I realized that I don't have to "buy her love" with goodies because we do so many other things together that are fun and not centered around eating.

Your grandchildren will love you just as much as long as you are a devoted grandmother. Let me make an important point, if you want to have a loving and trusting relationship with your children, then don't break their rules. So all you grandmas out there ask yourself if it is worth it to defy the wishes of the parents just to prove that you can. I know we want our grandchildren to think we are fun and special but this can be accomplished by going to their soccer games, taking them bowling, or to the movies and letting them plan the day when they are with you.

I must admit, when my grandchildren sleep over I do stock the pantry with their favorite cereals (sugar of course) that they don't get at home, along with mac and cheese boxes (must be Kraft's or they won't like it) and always take their "food orders" over the phone prior to their visit. Every so often I will let them have dessert before dinner, which they think is very cool. My daughter knows exactly what I am up to and is usually fine with it. Once in a while she will ask me not to take the "fast food" route because her son/daughter had just been to a party and ate too much junk food. I totally agree with her. I've learned in my many years as a parent, and in case you haven't noticed, when a child gets too much sugar in their system they can become moody and out of control due to being over stimulated, or they become very sluggish. If you are a new grandma or a grandma-to-be this is important to remember. For me, it took some time to sink in but I realized that I was contributing to my grandchild's eating habits, and not in a good way. However, I must admit that for a while I felt very sad that I could no longer be the "Candy man" or in this case, "Candy woman" in her life. The truth is, I am the one who is in love with sugar and somehow it seemed that it was fine to splurge for the sake of my grandchildren. I do not want to pass this addiction on to them. Again, everything in moderation means one Oreo cookie rather than three. And like any junkie, when you cut them off, they will argue. Be prepared. They may even roll out the big guns. When I cut off my granddaughter, she would say, "But Nana, you always gave me three cookies and besides, I can't finish my milk with just one!" And then she would give me that sad puppy-dog look. It worked for a while, I admit, until the day when I said, "I am on to you and that look."

Her response was, "Rats!"

My point being that we grandmothers need to create boundaries and stick to them. I had no idea that a three-year-old was capable of manipulating Nana.

But I now realize that the magic is in Nana, and not in the bag of Oreo cookies.

On the other hand, Bonnie my daughter-in-law, is totally into "organic only" and no processed foods. She and my son have very definite rules with regard to what foods their boys can eat. I love my daughter-in-law and consider her as my "daughter." We have a great relationship and can communicate honestly and freely with one another.

However, she and my son deflated my "Nana" balloon when they told me that I could not give my grandson anything processed, non-organic or sweets. I had been used to giving fun foods (they refer to them as junk foods) to my other grandchildren so this was tough for me to swallow. When they brought my grandson over they would bring his meals as well so I wouldn't have to worry about buying the right foods; actually, now that I think back on it, I think they didn't trust me.

After a while I began shopping at Whole Foods and buying organic fruits and vegetables not only for my grandson but for me and my husband as well. I now make sure to have organic apple juice, ketchup, and fruits when they come for dinner. I know they really appreciate it, and as my son said, "Mom, he loves being with you because you are fun and not because of what you feed him."

When Isaac, their son, was very young they never gave him sugary things. When he started pre-school one day the teacher handed out cookies. He took a bite, wrapped the rest in a napkin and took it home with him. As soon as his mom walked in the door, he ran over to her and said, "Mommy, you have to taste this; I got it from my teacher and it is so yummy that I had to share it with you!" So of course they allowed him to have sweets at school and birthday parties and special occasions. The interesting thing is that he doesn't like a lot of sweet treats. He does love chocolate but doesn't devour the entire cupcake or cookie like most kids do. He eats some icing then decides he wants to take the rest home. His mom told me he takes a few licks every day and is satisfied. I sure wish I could be like him, but it's too late now. My mom loved to bake so we had the most delicious desserts every night as far back as I can remember. I'm certainly not blaming her but hindsight is 20/20.

My sisters and I are definitely "sweet-a-holics" and all of us love to bake, but love the eating part the best. I can't believe it but as I am writing this all of a sudden I am craving something sweet to eat. There is much to be said about "the power of suggestion." If you are suddenly feeling the need for something sweet, go ahead. Indulge. I won't tell.

Sweets are one thing, but gifts can be another. When my grandchildren were toddlers I loved to bring them little presents when I saw them. Their excitement always warmed my heart. My son finally told me not to bring my grandson presents every time I visit because I was the present. He had a point because whenever I went to see my little guy he would first look behind my back and say, "Do you have a present for me?" So now I don't bring him a present every time, just once in a while, which is okay with his parents. The funny thing is that my son is now the stricter parent with what foods my grandson can and cannot have. He used to eat all kinds of "junk foods" growing up and when he went to the University of Pennsylvania, he always told me how great the steak and cheese subs were.

My "daughter," his wife, turned him into a "food Gestapo," and after all these years, she is now much more flexible. I took my grandson to lunch and a movie last week and was allowed to give him a chocolate chip cookie after he ate his lunch. I now ask my "daughter" if I can give him a treat, because she will let me. It's a level of trust that we've built together. And it helps that my grandson is on-board with the decisions we make together. It amazes me that my little five-year-old knows all about "healthy eating" and sticks to it.

So my final bit of advice to you is to honor the parents "life style" whether it be in the food department or otherwise. They may have a list or a schedule or rules, and they most likely will not agree with what you choose to do as a grandparent, but sometimes, you just have to let it go. After you get used to their ways and respect them you will feel good about yourself and how you have adapted to being flexible. This way everyone wins, and the grandchildren will visit you more and more.

# CHAPTER 10

# LESSONS LEARNED FROM GRANDMA

I have become proficient at playing *UNO* and I do not believe in letting my grandchildren win, though, if I am on a winning streak, I may lose one on purpose just to keep them interested. It's easy to enjoy being a winner but losing is another matter.

Life doesn't always go your way and I think it is important to expose them to this at an early age. The proof that I am doing the right thing is that when we are all playing a game and one of my grandchildren loses a few times, he or she sometimes gets angry and decides to quit. I step in with a quick, "no one wants to play with a quitter; remember that this is only a game" and then I spew out that tiresome phrase, "it's not whether you win or lose, but how you play the game." That's a tough one to swallow, even for adults, and I agree that it is fine to be competitive, but in the end it is about sportsmanship. Winning is easy but losing is something we all have to learn how to do gracefully. I am sure that after a three-hour tennis match, the loser has no desire to go to the net and congratulate his/her opponent, but they do because it is good sportsmanship.

Wait until you go to a few soccer games; there is always an obnoxious parent constantly yelling instructions to their kid or fighting with the referee for making a call they don't agree with. Not the greatest example to set.

And yes, grandmothers that are involved with their grandchildren have earned the right to teach them a few things. You will find that the parents are grateful that you set boundaries and are not afraid to give constructive criticism. The key word here is "afraid." Afraid that if you say no, or let them know they are doing or saying something that is unacceptable, you will no longer be their favorite grandmother. I felt this way when my first grandchild was born. I never wanted to disappoint her or say "no" to her for fear that she wouldn't think I was a "fun" Nana. I am sharing this with you in the hopes that you won't go through the "if I don't then she won't" phase of grandmotherhood.

Now that I am the proud Nana of five adorable, loveable, and sometimes aggravating grandchildren, I feel much more confident and therefore do not hesitate to reprimand bad behavior. Here is a perfect example; I had my three grandchildren (all siblings) over and we were having fun at breakfast until my grandson put the cereal box right in front of his sister's bowl. I asked him why he did that and he said it was because he didn't want to look at her because she had pimples and looked ugly. I was outraged, so I took his bowl of Frosted Flakes away, took him by the arm and demanded that he go upstairs to his room until he was ready to apologize. I scolded him for being so mean and for hurting his sister's feelings. Later I wondered if he would be upset with me and not think I was such a great Nana after all. I knew I did the right thing but wondered at what cost.

Later he came down and apologized to his sister and we all went on to play *UNO*. I guess I didn't think about the fact that his parents discipline him as well and he still thinks they are the best parents on the planet. So there you have it; it doesn't change a thing, except perhaps, bad behavior. But, be careful and pick your battles; after all, you are not the one who is totally responsible for raising them. Thank your lucky stars for that.

This brings up another sticky subject, so my friends, loosen up and listen. Do you allow your grandchildren to ask you why you have two chins or so many wrinkles on your face, even if it is true and they are just "telling it like it is"? Just because they're cute, cuddly and being totally honest, doesn't mean you have to ignore their insults. Remember the words of the great Aretha Franklin: *"R.E.S.P.E.C.T. GIVE IT TO ME, GIVE IT TO ME."* You go girl!

There is nothing wrong with teaching your grandchild that even honest questions can sting, and explain why. We've already discussed this in a previous chapter, but it begs to be mentioned again. And while we discussed the things that kids say to grandmothers, we left out Grandpa.

What should you do when they make fun of Grandpa because he has a big bald spot on the top of his head, or a pronounced round tummy, or hair sticking out of spots that usually don't have hair in younger people?

Absolutely nothing. He can fight his own battles if it bothers him.

My grandchildren always tease my husband about his bald spot; it doesn't bother him a bit. I think he has fun with it because once in a while he will put a sticker there and wait for the kids to notice. Then he acts as though he has no idea what they are talking about as he feels the top of his head in every place but where the sticker is. This cracks them up which is exactly what Grandpa intended to do.

# CHAPTER 11

# TO GRANDMOTHER'S HOUSE WE GO

I know how lucky I am to have all of my grandchildren living nearby so I won't pretend to tell you that you are wrong to feel abandoned when your children decide to move to another city or state and take your precious grandchildren with them. How can they do that to you? Well, unfortunately it's not about you. Once your son/daughter married and had a child they instantly became "a family."

Yes, you are a part of the family; hell, you even started the family by creating one of the key components, but now you have to step back, let your kids be adults, and make the best of it. It won't help to try and convince them not to move halfway across the country. Save your breath and try to figure out how best to handle this situation. Listen, don't be hard on yourself, you are going through the stages of mourning because not having them near you can be a tremendous loss. You know the classic five stages of grief, but the important one here is the last stage: acceptance.

You may have been asking yourself if it's even possible to maintain a close relationship with your children and grandchildren when they live in another state that is so far away. Though it is difficult, this depends on your state of mind. There are lots of things you can do to stay involved and maintain the closeness you had before they moved.

The most common way to stay close is through Skype or FaceTime. I just learned about it a few years ago and was blown away at how simple it is and that it doesn't even cost you extra money. You just hook up your computer with an application, or "app," as the kids call it these days, and that allows you to actually see your grandkids while talking to them. Both Skype and FaceTime can be used on smartphones, iPads, and most other tablets, and of course the computer. They will need to have the same application on their computer/device and no doubt your children will be happy to install one because, though you may not believe it, they feel it is just as important for their kids to have a relationship with their grandma as you do. Have a set time each week (we do Sunday early evening) when you Skype with your grandchild/grandchildren.

This will give all of you something to look forward to. If your grandchildren are little ones you can make a game out of it. Suggest that each week one of you gets to choose what to do; pick a book to read to them, and if they are older, decide on a book that they are interested in reading and then you can discuss it with them. It would be nice if you mailed them a copy with a little note from Grandma and some kisses. When I send anything to my grandchildren I always include my trademark: a happy face and a lipstick kiss.

As your grandchild gets older and can e-mail or text, then it will be even easier to keep in touch. My granddaughter has had an iPhone since she was six years old, and my fourteen-year-old granddaughter's computer skills are extremely advanced; she has even taught me a few things.

Times have certainly changed so use it to your advantage. If you let them know you are interested in them, you will find that they will reciprocate. When my children were young and went to overnight camp, I made sure they received a letter or a small package almost every day. That was a bit over the top and I am not suggesting that you do this every day, but if you get in the habit of sending them a little something once a month, they will love it. In exchange for this they have to promise to talk to you at least ten minutes each week by phone or Skype to let you know what their week was like and what they did. Yes, it is bribery, but so what; kids get very busy and though they love you they may think they have so many things going on that there is no time for "Grandma Time."

And whatever you do, do not tell your daughter/daughter-in-law that it is her responsibility to make sure the kids call Grandma. You have to be the one to call and ask them to help you set up a special time

Don't Call Me Grandma!

when you all can Skype, FaceTime, or have a phone conversation. Then let their mom know what they have said and confirm it with her.

Another option is for you to get used to planes, trains or automobiles, which make things much more palatable. Even though they live in another state you could still offer to visit them for a week and take care of the kids while mom and dad go on vacation. If you do, this earns you major points because they couldn't do this without you. What value do they place on having grandma come? It is PRICELESS!

Try to establish a "Grandma Visiting Schedule" that works for everyone; grandpa may even want to join you, though maybe not every time (this is fine so don't badger him or he will resent the trips). Whether or not you drive, take a train, or fly, they usually have rewards programs like frequent flier miles, and if you are of age, senior discounts help with the cost of travel. Both options are things that you should definitely look into. In exchange for your helping them out with a live-in babysitter during their trip, as well as being the one to travel to them, be sure to barter that with reciprocity. If you go to them, then you can set up certain holidays when they will all come to you. The other grandma and grandpa will want a holiday as well, I'm sure, so maybe even before your kids move, you can suggest the holiday that is most important to you and try to convince them that you have to have this agreement to help "lessen the pain and suffering" of them moving and taking your precious grandchild/children away from you.

There's nothing wrong with making them feel a little guilty for "upsetting the apple cart." I can tell you that friends of mine who have experienced this told me that the anxiety they felt prior to their children and grandchildren leaving was far worse than once it actually happened. Once the move was done, things calmed down and they fell into a routine (like I explained above), which made things a bit easier. I know you will still be forever saddened by the distance between you and them. I am not a therapist so my advice has no professional value; however, I have taken many surveys in the research for this book that have given me an overwhelming insight as to the emotions that go along with dealing with a long distance relationship with grandkids (as well as your son/daughter). However, if you can't seem to accept it without being constantly depressed, please seek out a therapist. Don't even try to explain how you feel to a close friend or your husband, they may try to help but no one truly knows how deep and real your feelings are except you.

When I was growing up, my mom gave me and my sisters our haircuts. We looked like she put a bowl over our head. But Mom always made things fun, so we didn't mind (until we were old enough to see what a mess she made of our hair). Mom used to have us call her on the phone and ask for Miss Rose, the beautician, to make an appointment. She instantly became Miss Rose and stayed in character until we left the basement. She had one of those hair dryers that stood on the floor and she used a card chair for us to sit on. We actually looked forward to visiting Miss Rose's Hair Salon; we loved the cookies she always served with a small glass of ginger ale.

I decided to follow in my mom's footsteps; not by cutting their hair, heaven forbid. When they sleep over I pretend that they are coming to "Nana's Hotel." I have rules posted on their bedroom door, which they think are very funny. I also leave chocolates on their pillow at night.

Here are Nana's rules:

# *NANA'S HOTEL RULES*

### *RULES MUST BE FOLLOWED:*

1. *Guests must brush their teeth in A.M. & P.M.*
2. *Guests under the age of 18 must go to bed on time*
3. *Guests must not fight or they will be locked away*
4. *Guests must not FART in bed; it will make other guests evacuate!!*

## Guests are entitled to the following:

1. **Toothbrush, toothpaste, towels, shower & bathtub**
2. **Toilet paper & soap**
3. **Clean sheets, pillow cases, soft & fluffy blankets**
4. **Licks from Charlie Brown, our dog**
5. **All the hugs and kisses they want**
6. **HAVING A GREAT TIME AT THE BEST HOTEL IN TOWN ... WHEN ROOMS ARE AVAILABLE! SO RESERVE THEM EARLY!**

**\*\*\* VIP GUESTS WILL GET CHOCOLATE KISSES ON THEIR PILLOW EVERY NIGHT \*\*\***

**DON'T FORGET TO PAY THE BILL WITH HUGS & KISSES TO THE OWNERS & TO LEAVE A BIG TIP FOR HOUSEKEEPING AND ROOM SERVICE**

# CHAPTER 12

# WHO IS NUMERO UNO?

Do you ignore your husband when you are with your grandchildren? Be very careful not to make him feel invisible. I have heard from some grandpas that when their grandchildren sleep over they become second citizens. It doesn't matter that your husband is also enjoying his role as grandpa; you want to grab all the attention because you think you have earned it. My children remember that when they slept at their Nana's house (my mom) before bedtime they always watched TV sitting between Nana and Grandpa. This part is fine because my husband and I do the same thing when our grandchild sleeps over. But, here's where the "acceptable" part ends with too many grandparents. When our grandchild falls asleep in our bed, my husband carries him/her to their room and tucks the little one into *their* bed.

My mom didn't want to disturb my kids, even though he/she would move around while sleeping and somehow end up with their feet practically in her face. So at this point she would lovingly ask my dad (poor Grandpa) to go sleep in the guest room. My dad went willingly, but you have to understand that he was so easy-going and always did whatever my mom asked him to do, with no resentment whatsoever.

I think my dad was one-of-a-kind. Although he was head of Obstetrics and Gynecology at Washington Hospital Center and had a stellar reputation, he was putty in the hands of my mom. Plus, he loved his grandchildren so much that I do believe he would have done anything for them. It was always, "Can I sleep at Nana's?" and not "Can I sleep at Nana's and Grandpa's house?" My grandchildren also say, "Can I sleep at Nana's Hotel?" but I have never, nor would I even consider asking my husband to sleep in the guest room. And if I did, well, let's just say he's no easy pushover. Plus, I would never want him to resent having our grandchild sleep over. Be aware of grandpa's feelings and try to include him in your plans. I guarantee you that he may agree to play *UNO* once or twice, but he won't want to sit there for hours playing games so let it be his choice, he will be much happier.

Are you known as the Granny who is always packing a huge photo book? There is nothing wrong with carrying a small "My Grandchildren" photo book in your purse. And for you tech-savvy grannies, who have file folders on your phone full of images of their bright, sweet faces, it's fun to share them as well. Good friends are truly interested and may even pull theirs out to share with you first. I know that when I go to lunch with my girlfriends we truly want to share pictures because we don't get to see one another's grandkids that often, and they change so much from one month to another when they are toddlers. However, we also have friends who get a bit carried away and bring a huge stack of photos to every lunch, as well as to dinner with other couples. I have seen men roll their eyes when a grandmother pulls out a bunch of photos thinking everyone at the table wants to see them. Don't be a "photo-packin' Granny" or your friends will definitely talk behind your back. And don't be surprised if they stop calling you to make plans. I have heard friends say, "What happened to Mary; she used to be so much fun and now she only wants to talk about her grandchildren!" Oh, and remember a very important rule; if you are out with a friend who is not yet a grandmother, never pull out the photo book unless asked. If you do, your friend most likely will be put off by this and perhaps even feel a bit resentful.

We all love our grandchildren dearly, but don't let them "rule the roost." Use your common sense, which sometimes goes out the window when we get blindsided by our adorable, precious, to die for grandchild. As I said in an earlier chapter, don't be afraid to use the "No" word. I know firsthand how difficult that is. Many times my granddaughter has asked me to take her to see a PG-rated movie. She always explains that she knows it is fine with her mom because they often go to PG-rated movies together. Well, the little rascal almost got me into deep trouble when I was about to agree. Then I thought twice and called her mom.

"Absolutely not!" was the response I got. I am sure if you were driving by my house that day, you would have heard her. So my granddaughter hung her head and gave me that "I'm so sorry I lied" look. And actually, if you stop and think for a moment, there is so much sex and violence even in some of the G-rated movies these days, so it pays to be aware.

I am appalled by the amount of violence kids are exposed to. I took my little one to see *Puss N Boots* a few months ago. That sword-wheeling cat was fighting in every scene. In fact, everyone was fighting. I only started noticing that this is a reoccurring theme in Disney movies as well. Just because it's animated doesn't mean that it's for children. Pay attention.

I don't think I am old fashioned, but these days there is so much violence in our world, in our neighborhoods, and on TV, that I wish movie producers would steer clear of the violence. Animation has even been taken to another level, some filled with violence and or inappropriate language. I just want to say that you really have to clear your grandchild's choice of movies with their mom. Our grandchildren may be *numero uno* in our world, but sometimes, you still have to think about *numero dos, tres, quatro* and everyone else around that child or children. As a grandparent,

I may see a movie first and report to their mom as to whether or not I think it is appropriate. My advice is always very much appreciated, however I try not to let my grandkids know that I reported to mom; that would make me the bad guy by preventing them from seeing a certain movie. Me, the bad guy? Not if I can prevent it. My daughter knows how I feel and would never sell me out. After all, I love my grandchildren, and I do what I do to protect them.

# CHAPTER 13

# WHAT ABOUT GRANDPA?

I decided to add this chapter because my husband, Norm, otherwise known as Grandpa, is a great role model for all grandfathers. Norm has such fond memories of his own grandfather, who sadly passed away when our children were very young. Norm called him Grandpa Morris, which is why he decided that he wanted to be called "Grandpa" as well. To this day Norm still talks about how his Grandpa Morris always made him laugh.

When our first grandchild, Jaclyn Rose, was born, Norm officially became Grandpa and couldn't wait until she was old enough to notice his silliness and laugh at him. No one made Jaclyn laugh more than her Grandpa. He would have her giggling out loud for hours. Then came Cole, Camryn, and Isaac who also think "Grandpa is so funny!" Of course, this warms Norm's heart and encourages him to do ridiculous things, which in turn brings more giggles. When I asked Jaclyn what was so funny about Grandpa and she said the funniest thing that Norm says is "When

Grandpa tells us he was in the major leagues and was in the Baseball Hall of Fame." This is something that they have always questioned and laughed when he insisted he was.

And, of course, every Halloween he bites off the white part of a candy corn and quickly holds his mouth and moans "oh, no! Look, my tooth came out!" as he boldly displays the top of the candy corn. After years of this they now think Grandpa is corny yet they still try to do "the candy corn thing" before he thinks to do it, but of course, it doesn't stop him; he just moans louder.

Another one of his favorite things to do when he is being "Grandpa" (and unfortunately, now sometimes when he is just with me) is to walk into a candy shop and with his most serious face and ask, "Do you know where I can buy some candy?" And believe it or not, most of the time the salesperson very seriously says, "Yes, we sell it." He does this in doughnut shops as well. I always pipe in saying, "sorry, he thinks he is funny," and at that point the salesperson smiles the "now I get it" smile.

When our children were growing up, I always let them skip school on their birthday and pick what they wanted to do. Now, Grandpa takes each grandchild out on a "special date" (just the two of them) and also lets them pick where they will go. This has been something that they all think about for months, trying to decide on plans. Their dates range from trips to the zoo, museums, theatre, sporting events, etc. Now that they are getting a little older, their selections are definitely more mature and sometimes surprising. Grandpa has always been a history buff and has shared this with our grandchildren when they became old enough to understand. He usually begins by saying, "When I fought in the Civil War ..."

When Cole was eight he decided he wanted to see a Civil War re-enactment so Grandpa drove him three-and-a-half hours to see it. It was a steamy hot summer day so when they finally arrived to see the show, after 20 minutes Cole turned to Grandpa and said, "Grandpa, I am sweltering out here, can we please go inside." So of course that's what they did. Grandpa bought him a hot dog and a REAL sword that Cole wanted. Then Cole asked if they could leave (even though they had driven over three hours to get there!) Norm was a little disappointed but Grandpa just smiled and said, "Cole, this is your day so let's go."

When they got home I asked what was the best part of their day and he said, "The sword Grandpa bought me and getting candy from his stash." He did say that on the drive to see the re-enactment Grandpa explained what the Civil War was all about. Cole loves history and remembers everything he learns.

Later, Norm turned to me and said, "I could have told him about the Civil War, bought him a hotdog and a sword at Toys R Us and he would have been happy! But he wanted to see the re-enactment so I guess I couldn't get out of the six-hour round trip car ride."

That's Grandpa for you.

Because Jaclyn is the oldest of our grandkids, she was the first one to go on a "Grandpa Date." She picked many of her favorite places but when I asked her which date was her favorite, she immediately smiled and said, "I couldn't believe he was able to get us tickets to an *American Idol* concert. We had a fun dinner first and when we got to the convention center he asked me what I wanted him to buy for me. I got the *American Idol* T-shirt, which was so cool! We had an amazing time!"

The year Jaclyn turned 11-years-old she decided she wanted Grandpa to take her to a fancy restaurant. So, Norm made a reservation downtown in D.C. near the White House. Unfortunately, the weather was terrible that night so Grandpa took Jaclyn to Ruth's Chris, which is nearby. Jaclyn ordered a Caesar Salad and a steak with French fries and to top it off they shared two desserts. During dinner Grandpa asked Jaclyn what she was studying in school. She said she was learning about the American Revolution, so they talked about it for a while. Jaclyn had "an amazing time" and felt so grown up. Grandpa said he was surprised at how much Jaclyn knew about the revolution and how eager she was to discuss it with him. This is a perfect example of why it is such a treat to take each grandchild out separately; you will really get to know what she/he is all about.

He often would come to their schools for classroom concerts and programs, as well as multiple sporting events. He even stood outside in the snow and freezing cold to watch Cole's seven-year-old flag football championship. The kids all know that anything they want to know about the world "just ask Grandpa, he knows everything."

He engages them on their level as well as instructs them to learn about history and politics and the important things in life. Unfortunately, Jaclyn has had to undergo many surgeries in her 14 years; and Grandpa has been there for each one. He was always there to support Lisa and Scott and, of course, Jaclyn, his first precious grandchild.

Camryn went on her first date with Grandpa when she was four. She chose to go to a Wizard's basketball game in D.C. She said, "The best part of our date was getting cotton candy and Grandpa being funny and of course, that he bought me whatever I wanted!" I asked her what he did that made her laugh. She started to laugh again and said, "While we were watching the game Grandpa looked at me and burped out loud. I couldn't stop laughing; he was so funny! And then he told a funny joke and I laughed again. It's fun to have a funny Grandpa because he is always silly and sometimes too silly and that cracks me up."

When Camryn was five, she wanted to go to the zoo for her date with Grandpa. It was a very hot summer day and the zoo has a lot of hills. I asked her all about the date and she explained how Grandpa made it a special day.

"Grandpa kept saying, 'Ugh, I'm so old, I can't walk anymore,' at the top of every hill. He was funnier than the animals, except the ape because we saw him poop. Then Grandpa said 'it's a good thing he didn't poop on my head!' which made me laugh again.

He is so, so funny! Oh, and of course, I love to get candy from the stash in his car. I love candy so much and when I am with Grandpa I can eat as much as I want; well, almost as much as I want.

Another great thing about my Grandpa is that he takes us on the best trips. For Nana's birthday she wanted us all to go on a cruise together. Grandpa took us all on the Disney Ship at Christmas."

I asked Cole what he liked most about Grandpa. He thought for a moment and then explained what he enjoyed about his time with Grandpa.

"Well, there are a lot of things," Cole said, "but one thing is that Grandpa can always answer my questions because he knows everything, so I know I can ask him something and he will know the answer. Also, Grandpa is very thoughtful and loves to have fun. He is hilarious when he does the 'Gangnam' Style Dance. We all couldn't stop laughing."

When Isaac turned four, it was time to go on a "Grandpa date." He was very excited and immediately said he wanted Grandpa to take him to the Air and Space Museum. My son, Brian, interviewed Isaac for me when he returned from their date. As usual, he had lots to say. The following paragraphs are direct quotes from our little Isaac.

"I saw all kinds of really, really cool airplanes. Grandpa told me that those kinds of airplanes go speeding away really fast! Then I saw a spaceship bigger than our house! I had so much fun with Grandpa at the Museum. I holded Grandpa's hands at the museum. I saw a souvenir place and Grandpa said of course we'll get a souvenir but after we see all the cool airplanes.

"Grandpa taught me that air pushes out of the back of the space shuttle and that makes it go fast. When Grandpa was a kid he said he only had a plain fire truck to play with. No hoses, just a red fire truck; not like my fire trucks. The best part was when Grandpa bought me my space shuttle. It wasn't expensive, so I wanted it because I thought it would be cool to have an airplane that has things that open and close (referring to the storage bay doors on the top).

"I had the best time with Grandpa. I don't know what Grandpa's daddy's name is because he might be in heaven because Grandpa was a kid a long time ago."

Then Brian asked him what his favorite things are about Grandpa.

"My favorite thing to do with Grandpa is to go to the space museum," Isaac admitted. "I like going to places with him. I like it when Grandpa is silly! I like playing at his house with Charlie (our dog) and eating at his house. I always have the best time when it's just me, Nana, Grandpa, and you and mommy. I like to do interlocking fingers with Grandpa. He does a good job being my Grandpa and takes care of me and I never get lost and Grandpa is funny."

Brian asked Isaac to describe what Grandpa looks like.

"He looks like you but has a different voice but he has light brown hair like me. He doesn't have a lot of hair. He has a hole in his head for his hair and it's not connected to the hair on the sides."

And that about sums up Grandpa.

CHAPTER 14

# HOW TO BE A TECH-SAVY GRANDMOTHER

You know what our kids learned about dinosaurs? They learned that dinosaurs lived long, long ago in another world and they are now extinct. Replicas and fossilized bones can only be found in museums. In order for your grandchildren not to think that you are from "long, long ago" and that you know nothing about their world, you not only have to dress and act cool (as I mentioned earlier) and be familiar with their trends, music, etc. but it is mandatory to be a "Tech-Grandma." This will score you big points with the young ones, and will actually make you feel smart because you have learned their ways.

It was a rude awakening the day I realized that my young grandkids knew how to watch a show they missed on TV by going to "On Demand," when I couldn't even remember the term, much less know how to do it. I had to secretly ask my husband what it meant and to teach me. Between you and me, I still have trouble understanding how it all works, but my grandkids don't know that. I make it a point to say, "Oh, if you haven't seen -------, you can go to On Demand."

They look at me wide-eyed and I know they are thinking, "Wow, Nana really knows a lot!"

Another important point: it is imperative that you learn how to use a computer (you will find that almost every classroom has one, even in some pre-schools). At first I was totally intimidated each time I sat in front of my new computer. I sabotaged myself by thinking I could never learn to use it, nor should I have to. When my first granddaughter, who, at the age of seven, became proficient at it, I began to think that I was too old to learn. I decided to improve my image.

I was determined to become a "tech-savvy Nana," even if it killed me. So I took a few private lessons and was on my way. It wasn't so scary after all.

Now, don't let me overwhelm you with all this new technology; by the time I finish this book you will probably already know this stuff and then there will be more "stuff" to learn because technology is constantly changing. In fact, by the time you finish reading this book, your new computer, tablet and smart phone may be obsolete. It happens so fast.

So, everyone around me was "texting," which I thought was absurd. E-mailing is certainly fast enough and don't you hate turning on your computer and finding a million e-mails from people and companies you never heard of? How annoying can this stuff get?

It's crazy that everyone is so obsessed with it all. But, I guess you "can't fight city hall," as the saying goes. Even my friends and contemporaries were texting me. For months I would tell them: "I do not text so either pick up the phone (what's a phone?) or if you must, then send me an e-mail." I held out as long as I could and just got sick of hearing, "what do you mean you don't text?" It felt like it was a cardinal sin. So once again, if you can't beat them, join them, which seemed to always bite me in the ass if I tried to refuse. If you don't join them, you really do feel like an outcast. So, now I also text, and everyone (friends and grandkids) said it was about time.

I remember when my husband bought me my first Blackberry; I thought I would never learn all the things it was capable of. Unfortunately, once I became comfortable with it, BlackBerrys became extinct. I only hoped that wouldn't happen to me. I felt like technology was attacking me at every turn. Everyone had iPhones, even my grandkids! Was I frustrated? You bet your sweet tech *#@ I was!

So once again I gave in, or I should say, I gave up. I have to laugh because once I had the iPhone 4 my granddaughter said I should definitely trade it in for an iPhone 5. I wanted to say, "GIVE ME A FRIGGIN BREAK!"

But instead I just smiled and told her that I was doing fine with the iPhone 4. I guarantee you that by the time you are reading this book there will probably be an iPhone 12 which will only communicate with those who also have one. Get wise and wake up consumers, as long as we continue to buy the "latest and greatest" the companies laugh all the way to the bank and come up with another "must have" addition.

So, I told you earlier about "Nana's Hotel Rules" and now I am going to tell you about my "techno-rules." These are the rules that I expect my grandkids to adhere to when we are out in public, at a restaurant or a movie theater, or even shopping. The rules are simple, and I do enforce them. I am especially vigilant when we go to a restaurant.

- No iPhones
- No texting
- No iPod Touch
- No iPads
- No laptop computers
- No headphones
- No listening to music

They may not like my rules, and I know it is tough for them, but I find other ways to keep them busy until their food arrives. We used to play "Hangman," or "20 Questions," or "I Spy," when they were younger. Now it seems they are always plugged into something. I have noticed that even when they are with a friend they are still doing something on their iPods/iPhones/iPads; together, but NOT together. They call this a playdate? Not in my book!

When I pick them up to take them to a movie or the mall, or anywhere, actually, I do not allow them to do any of the above. Guess what, they find it difficult to carry on a conversation without being "plugged in." I explained to my grandkids that I don't get to spend much time with them anymore because they all have after school and weekend sports. Do you ever feel like the English language is passé? How sad, because when they grow up and get jobs they won't have the social skills to communicate with their boss or co-workers. This is a fact I actually read about in an article with regard to our younger generation and the obstacles they will have to deal with as young adults. Even their parents are texting every minute so what do you expect?

Everything moves at such a fast pace in today's world so I suppose working parents have to keep up. We were out to dinner last week enjoying each other and catching up when my son's iPhone began to ring, and, of course, he had to step away from the table to take the call (some people are not that considerate and will talk on their phones with no regard for others in the restaurant). It was his boss calling to ask him to work on an emergency document that evening and to send it to him as soon as possible. This seems to be the "norm" these days. I guess our grandchildren see this all the time so they mimic their parents by wanting to be "plugged in" as well.

It is okay for you to set boundaries when they are with you; they won't like it at first so don't cave. Be strong and stick to your guns. Now my grandkids understand that when they are with me we actually talk to one another and play word games to keep them occupied while waiting for their food to be served. Once in a while my oldest granddaughter will ask me if she can please text a friend because it is of the utmost importance (according to her). So I say "sure honey." I don't want to be the *wicked* grandmother about it, so I do let them use their "stuff" while driving someplace that may take more than ten minutes to reach.

As I re-read the above paragraph, I realized that it may come across as me being a bit of a "control freak," but I do cherish the times I have with my grandchildren, and they do understand why I make and enforce these rules. So, again, make sure you are "fun" and seem interested in "their world as they see it." Seeing the world through their eyes, with the unprecedented amount of technology at their disposal is the key to really bonding with them.

I asked my oldest granddaughter, Jaclyn, who is now fourteen (going on eighteen), to bring me up to speed on the "texting language" that the kids use. So here are a few "abrevs," (which is an abbreviation of the word, abbreviation) as they call it, and, according to her, use **only** lower case letters.

. bff – best friends forever
- lol – laugh out loud
- brb – be right back
- gtg – got to go

- luv – love
- u – you
- ttyl – talk to you later
- 2 moro – tomorrow
- 2 nite – tonight
- btw – by the way
- gr8 – great
- ily – I love you
- idk – I don't know
- wat – what
- r – are
- y – why
- plz – please
- ilysm – I love you so much

And there are many, many more, and new ones are created everyday. I never was very good at learning languages so I have to have a "cheat sheet" next to me when texting my granddaughter, but she thinks I am very cool because I know her language and use it.

**"Btw, wat r u up 2 2moro?"**
**"idk, ttyl, gtg!"**
**"ily"**
**"ily2"**

While it may look like Greek (it certainly did to me), this is actually a full-fledged conversation between two people. Here is the translation:

"By the way, what are you up to tomorrow?"
"I don't know, talk to you later, got to go."
"I love you."
"I love you too."

This is their take on the English language. The next generation's technology-based language, written in a series of jumbled letters. I wonder what will happen when they have to write a book report, or a business proposal. Do you think they will answer an exam question by writing "idk"? But if you use the above "abrevs" your grandkids will have a new level of respect for you and guess what? It can actually make you feel young and in the loop. So, my advice would be to start memorizing. Or, carry a small cheat sheet like this Nana does. lol.

CHAPTER 15

# MOTHERS VS. GRANDMOTHERS: THE ETERNAL STRUGGLE, AND HOW TO GET OVER IT

I decided that in order for you, the grandmother, to understand things that you can do (or not do) differently, it would be necessary for me to interview the moms. Everything that was told to me was in the strictest of confidence so I must honor thy moms, even if I think some of them are full of crap and found some of what they said to be utterly ridiculous. I am, of course, a grandmother so maybe I was a bit defensive while reading some of their "requests" or even "demands" in some cases. But, we, as grandmothers, do have to suck it up because, as I said earlier, we are no longer in the proverbial driver's seat.

How sad that is.

In our defense, we did a darn good job in raising our kids but they don't get it, they still think we're clueless. Yes, we know times have changed but what the hell; why take away our credibility? Okay, having said all that, I will now honor "thy moms" and tell their side.

First, I want to tell you some personal changes that were required of me by my daughter/daughter-in-law in order for me to earn my place as "a wonderful Nana." I did learn a lot and won't lie to you, I had hurt feelings along the way, but I must admit that a lot of my actions as a mom did need some revamping. That's a nice way of saying that, as I had to learn to keep my mouth shut and if you know me (and after 14 chapters, I hope you know me), you would understand how difficult that is, for I am definitely "don't speak now" challenged. My dad was a doctor and my mom was a "doctor by osmosis," so naturally I am as well. When our first granddaughter, Jaclyn Rose, was born to our loving, bright, and beautiful daughter and handsome and smart son-in-law (just in case he is reading this, but it is the honest truth) Jaclyn was a pound-and-a-half, the size of a small Beanie Baby and this is no exaggeration. She, unfortunately, had many health issues and spent the first four months of her life at Children's Hospital in Washington, D.C. Lisa and Scott handled the situation better than most parents could have. They were always very positive and Lisa never left Jaclyn alone. She and Scott were, and still are, truly amazing parents.

So, you ask, how did I get in trouble?

Whenever any of my children were ill, I always asked the doctor a million questions and still do to this day. We were all waiting in a conference room at the hospital to speak to Jaclyn's doctor, when he finally came in the room and began to explain Jaclyn's condition I must have interrupted a few times to ask questions, reason being that I am always afraid that if I wait, I will definitely forget what I wanted to ask. Well, I really stepped into the lion's den without a shield. I was scolded and was told that if I couldn't be quiet I would not be allowed to sit in anymore. Obviously, nerves were frazzled so I was reprimanded in a very unpleasant way. I did promise not to open my mouth again and told myself that because they were so upset and worried about their baby they didn't realize how harshly they were speaking to me.

Later that day, Lisa did apologize for the way she spoke to me and as we hugged, I told her I understood and was not upset with her, just the situation. Here's the big lesson I learned; if I am quiet and wait until the doctor is finished speaking and wait until Lisa asks her questions, my concerns are usually addressed. That was 14-years ago, but I did learn to let my daughter ask her questions first, and to my amazement, she asked all the right ones in detail. When she was finished and the doctor has answered her questions, Lisa then turned to me and asked if I had any questions.

So, by learning to listen, through the years, I am now always by their side whenever Jaclyn sees her doctors. This also taught me how to be "the observer," which is a totally different role for me but one that works very well. I do a lot more "observing" with friends and family and have learned to put myself in their shoes. I must say, I am damn proud of myself for toeing the line and being fine with it.

Last week I went with my daughter and granddaughters to see *Parental Guidance,* which is a must-see movie for all grandparents and their daughters/daughter-in-laws. By the time you are reading this you will have to get it on Netflix, but trust me, it is so worth it. Billy Crystal and Bette Midler are the grandparents and are asked by their daughter to stay with their kids so they can get away. I can stop here because the movie's title says it all.

Then there is my wonderful daughter-in-law and my wonderful son. I have to say that I feel more like a mother to Bonnie than a mother-in-law because I love her as though she were my daughter. She and my son Brian are total health nuts (pardon the expression) and I am sure that is a good thing most of the time. At first it was difficult for me to understand why "Nana" couldn't take her grandson to McDonalds once in a while. However, now that Isaac is five, they have become much more flexible as to what Isaac can and cannot eat. He knows what is healthy and now prefers to eat the healthy stuff, but still loves his French fries. Bonnie and Brian do let me buy a cookie for him and the funny thing is that he takes a few bites and saves the rest. Oh how I wish that would rub off on me, but not in this lifetime. When Isaac was younger, most of the time when he would come to Nana's to eat; Bonnie and Brian would bring his food. This really made me unhappy, so I have promised to go to Whole Foods to be totally organic and always ask exactly what I should buy when they come for dinner, etc. If I offer Isaac something he isn't sure he should have, he always says, "Will Mommy let me have this?" Of course, he is a little boy and still tries to get me to give him French fries, but truly, I will give him a few after he eats his broccoli. I am not just saying this because I know Brian and Bonnie will be reading every word of this. They know I abide by their rules and honestly, the main reason is because Isaac will report back to his mom everything I give him. Remember what I said earlier (this is worth repeating), never say to your grandchild, "I will give this to you if you promise not to tell your mom." You can bet that whatever "forbidden fruit" you gave him/her, even though you both did a pinkie swear, will be the first thing that comes out of the kid's mouth when mom opens the door and says, "Did you have fun with grandma?" Yes, you will be totally screwed.

It is easy to discuss likes and dislikes with your daughter, but most of the time it is very difficult to be that open with your daughter-in-law. I am very lucky because from the get-go, Bonnie and I made a pact that we would always tell each other what is on our mind. And the most important thing is NOT to do it through e-mails because the tone is usually misunderstood.

She and I have a set date to meet for breakfast once a month to discuss what's going on with us. I am so lucky and cherish the time I can spend alone with her. If we are upset about something, we pick up the phone. I do understand that this won't work for every relationship but it never hurts to try. I am more flexible with Bonnie and Brian because I have to be in order to keep the peace, and for all of us to truly be happy with one another. With my daughter, Lisa, I can fight for what I want to do, and sometimes I win and other times I lose, but for the most part Lisa lets me be the "Nana" I have always wanted to be.

Now it is time to tell it like it is with many young moms that I interviewed. I found that the complaint I heard most often was that they wished their mom/mother-in-law would be a more involved grandmother. It seems that many grandmothers visit only when it is convenient for them and do not play an active role in their grandchildren's life. As you know, in today's world our grandchildren are involved in after-school activities as well as activities on weekends. Another complaint that was expressed by so many moms is that grandmothers are not present at most of their kid's activities. They want us to be more present and to offer to help with carpooling and to ask how we can help them. Think about it and really listen to what's going on because almost every mom told me they do not want to ask for the grandmother's involvement and are disappointed and hurt because grandma is not proactive and they feel grandma should WANT to be a part of what's going on with their grandkids.

One mom I interviewed was totally stressed when she breast fed her first child and was always exhausted. She said her mom would come over and she could not understand why her daughter was so stressed.

"What's the big deal? Get a bottle!" she said one time, which only made matters worse. However, the positive things she had to say about her mom far outweighed the negative. Though her mom expects perfect manners, "we speak, eat, walk and dress this way" her children still adore their grandmother and have even put her on a Grandma pedestal. This is because she always makes sure that when her grandkids come to visit she has all of their favorite shows on DVR, all of their favorite foods in the pantry, and always spends a lot of time helping them with reading, school work, or whatever is appropriate for their age. However, she does refuse to help with potty training, but still supports her daughter by telling her she is doing a great job.

Another complaint that was told by many moms is that their moms criticize them for not having their child potty trained by a certain age. And many say, "You were completely potty trained by this age," implying that they are not doing a good job. No young mom wants to be compared to your parenting skills unless it is all-positive, so remember to compliment, compliment, and compliment; if the mom is happy then most likely grandma will be as well. Also, many have told me that their moms do not follow the list of instructions when they drop their child off to stay at grandma's house. I never said a word, but come on moms! Do you really have to give us a three-page list of what to do and what not to do every time our grandkids visit? I know some grandmothers that cringe at the list handed to them and most of the time ignore it anyway. If the child has health issues or is a baby, I get it; but really, if you don't trust us then don't ask us to babysit. Even though it would break our hearts.

Here is another mom's story, reprinted as it was sent to me, and one in which I found to be very sad:

"I am sharing this with you anonymously!

My grandmother picked me up from school every Friday; we went to Capital Bakery for a black and white cookie. Then we would play Old Maid or Chutes and Ladders until it was time to get ready for family Shabbat.

We lit candles together and sang Jewish choir songs together. We played beauty parlor and she taught me things like always start at the bottom when you are buttoning something. My grandmother bought me an Easter Basket every year, just because I was her bunny!

My grandmother made me sour cream and cottage cheese with bananas and sugar!

I have an abundance of sweet memories of my grandma, who I sadly lost at the age of thirteen. My husband and I pay for every second of help we have for our three children.

Both grandmothers live in the same town; however they have no special rituals or even special time with our kids for that matter! They attend school functions if it's convenient.

My mother missed four years of my daughters dance recitals. With a plethora of activities to choose from, maybe my mother comes to two of my son's games a year, maybe. It saddens me, and I believe it is disappointing for my kids as well, to miss out on having that special bond with someone like a grandmother.

I hope when I am so lucky to become a grandmother that I will have an open heart and calendar to bring those traditions back as only a grandmother can."

Here is another mom's response:

"I don't have much to say about my Mom except that I wish she could spend more time with my kids. As for my Mother-in-law, I have to say I am also very lucky. She knows when to step in and when to hold back when it comes to anything to do with my family. The one thing I wish she would not do is parent my children. She will talk to them in a very parental way (tone and discipline) instead of just being that person in their lives that loves them unconditionally and enjoys them.

She will often try to discipline and point out right from wrong and push for them to do more (i.e. school work, read) using a parental tone rather than a matter of fact loving grandparental tone.

A perfect way to explain this is, my mother will show up with an article about a movie or a new magic trick or any item that pertains to whatever my kids are interested in at the time. She will sit with them and talk about their lives and really actively listen to them. My mother in law shows up with a math practice workbook; if my kids are in the car with her she will make a pit stop along the way to see all the other people she needs to see that day. She has gotten better about the "stopping by" because I sat down and asked her to please stay for longer and spend time more time which she took to heart, to her credit, and now will stay for dinner."

I guess the lesson to be learned here is to understand that we were mothers once too, and what worked for us may not work for the new generations. The world is a much different place now, and, as grandparents, we have to be aware of not only our wishes and desires when it comes to our grandchildren, but also take into account the wishes and desires of the parents. It's a hard lesson to learn, trust me on that. But when that happy balance is achieved, all parties involved will benefit.

So, talk to your kids, and listen. Listen to them and I'm pretty sure you will find that common ground. The end result will be happy grandkids, and isn't that what we all want anyway?

# CHAPTER 16

# GRANDMA HAS GONE TO HEAVEN, OR MAYBE BOCA: WHAT TO TELL A CHILD

How do you tell your child that Grandma is no longer with us? I am not a therapist and do not pretend to be one. So if you are having difficulty in explaining what happens when someone you love passes away, it probably is a good idea to see a therapist, or check out some web sites that deal with grief.

Kids are a lot smarter than you think. Don't try to sugarcoat the loss of their grandmother by making up a story to protect them. Don't tell them that Grandma moved to France, Boca, or anywhere else that is some distance away. Just because they are three- or- four years-old, does not mean that you should lie to them; they will find out somehow, and then trust can, and will, become an issue.

Unfortunately, my wonderful daughter-in-law lost her mom unexpectedly, which was traumatic for all of us. However, she lived in Florida and we all live in

Maryland. Every Sunday my grandson, Isaac, would Skype with Grandma, and though she lived far away, they were very close. They also talked on the phone, and when Grandma came to visit we all had so much fun being together.

My grandson was only two when his Grandma died. That evening Bonnie and Brian told Isaac that "something very sad has happened. Grandma died because her body stopped working and she is in Heaven."

Bonnie read him a book called *I Miss You* and repeatedly answered his questions about Heaven. She went into great detail. When we flew down to Florida, Isaac came with us but stayed with a close friend during the funeral service. We were all in shock and though my daughter-in-law was in excruciating pain, she was able to hide it from her son.

Bonnie is a wonderful therapist by trade, so I asked her how she handled crying in front of Isaac.

"I normalized his feelings and at times when I cried in front of him, I explained why I was crying. The message to communicate is to balance being a good model of expressing emotions while not falling apart (e.g., sobbing uncontrollably) in front of a young child."

Since his Grandma passed away, Bonnie and Brian take Isaac to the cemetery on a regular basis because they continue to fly to Florida and now are emotionally able to stay in Grandma's apartment. Of course, Isaac doesn't know that bodies are buried in the cemetery, just that it is a place to remember people who have gone to Heaven.

One day, a new Whole Foods opened near Bonnie and Brian's house, so the three of them went to see the new organic grocery store. When they walked in, Bonnie looked around and exclaimed, "This is Heaven!" Isaac immediately looked up at her with a smile and asked, "Is Grandma here?" Taken aback, Bonnie had to explain why she felt the store was "like Heaven" because heaven is such a peaceful and beautiful place. Then there were questions like, "Can I go to Heaven to see Grandma?"

When Bonnie told me what Isaac had said, I asked her how she responded to his question.

"I answered empathically, but also practically," Bonnie explained, "letting him know that we cannot go to Heaven while we are still alive. I also realized the value of avoiding euphemisms!"

Bonnie has written many books. Because the book *I Miss You* is for four-to-eight-year-olds who had experienced losing someone, she decided to write a book for two-to-three-year-olds called *Something Very Sad Happened*, which also offers guidance for parents and caregivers. This book will be released very soon.

Bonnie also told me about a wonderful website that has a long list of reading/resources dealing with death. It is The Wendt Center for Loss and Healing, **www.wendtcenter.org**. Look under "Resources" and "In Print."

I wasn't sure whether or not to write this chapter, for the simple reason that I want this book to be a fun, yet informative read. But let's face it, we all have to go sometimes and I don't mean on vacation to Boca! When my time comes (hopefully not for a very long time) I know my grandchildren will be told the truth. Actually, I have mentioned to them that Nana won't always be here and have asked them what they want me to leave them. We play a game of taking turns to tell Nana what they want.

Before my mom died, when she was very healthy, she had my sisters and me over one afternoon. We thought we were going to have a yummy lunch (she was a great cook) but she had other intentions. Of course, we did have a delicious lunch followed by her famous Coconut Cake. Then she brought out a bowl with folded pieces of paper in it. We had no idea what we were about to do. She smiled and told us that we were going to take turns picking the folded papers which would then be what each of us would inherit after she was gone. How depressing. We truly didn't want to think about it. But my mom was always cracking jokes and immediately put the "death" part aside and the game began.

Mom said we could trade our papers if we wanted to. We actually had fun trying to out-bid one another if two of us wanted the same thing. That afternoon was a lot of fun; never did we think that Mom would leave us two years later. I can tell you this: her idea was a brilliant one. When the time came to divide her belongings, it had already been done. I will do the same thing with my children. I already typed the distribution of my personal things and left everyone something special. This is not a morbid thing to do when you are still healthy and far from leaving this earth. It's truly planning ahead so everyone benefits with the least amount of grief and to make sure that everyone is equally taken care of.

This is just a suggestion, and something that worked for my family and me. Each person will have his or her own way to deal with the inevitable loss, and no one way is the right or wrong way to do it. Just be honest with your young ones and you can avoid trust issues later on. But no matter how you do it, make sure that you let them know that they are loved, and that Grandma will always be with them. My grandmas are still both with me. You've read about them in these pages.

That's how I keep their memories alive.

My good friend, Laney Oxman, lost her mother-in-law some years ago. She sent me the following:

"When my granddaughter, Ila Rose, was nine, my husband's mother (her GreatGrandmother) passed away. Last year (Ila was ten) she wrote a poem to Grandma Min that I would like to share."

## GRANDMA MIN

I miss you with all my heart,
Where you are right now, can
you see me part by part?
Is it weird to be up so high?
It was hard to say good bye.
In the heavens are there lemons sweet and sour
Pink with powder?
You're the one, you're the best,
I think about you in every test.
Do you see the clouds, do you see the crowds?
Are you so proud, do you miss the ground?
Can you see the eagles, can you see the beagles?
Will you come down one day to see us play?
And don't worry, I will never forget you.
You're in my heart and that's where I see you.
Love, Ila

Bogart, Ila, Grandma Laney

# CHAPTER 17

# DON'T CALL ME GRANDMA ...

Now that I have shared my thoughts with regard to Grannies from years past and how we modern Grandmas, Mimis, Nanas, etc,. are so different, I hope you can understand why I gave birth to this little yellow book. At my age, it's about the only birthing I can do; and I promise you, the delivery took way more than nine months!

As I mentioned in chapter one, becoming a grandmother today is definitely a life-altering experience that defines us in a whole new light. Hopefully, it's a bright light; one of my favorite songs from our generation is Debby Boone's "You Light Up My Life." This is what grandkids do and why we are so fortunate to have them. Yet, as I mentioned, probably a million times, there are plenty of bumps in the road for all of us. Choices are not always available, which is a tough pill to swallow. I believe Mary Poppins said it best, "A spoonful of sugar makes the medicine go down in the most delightful way."

Two key words to remember are *Recognition* and *Submission*. If we're treated with respect, it's easier to submit to our children's requests, rather than demands. It's all a matter of semantics; it's not what you say but how you say it. This applies to us, our children, and even our grandchildren.

When I decided to write the Grandparents' Bill of Rights, my intention was for this to be a wake-up call to our children to let them know that we should not be demoted to "second class citizens" just because we no longer are in control when it comes to raising our grandchildren. Believe me, it's a pleasure to sit back and enjoy the ride, once we know how to navigate the bumps along the way. There should be a prep course, GRANDMOTHERHOOD 101. It certainly would prepare us for learning how to step down gracefully, as well as how to maintain our voice. Laryngitis may occur but if given the proper tools, we will learn how to regain our voice in an acceptable balance.

I repeat, this WAS my intention; then the proverbial light bulb flickered so brightly, causing the birth of a new idea. Maybe, just maybe, I should hear the other side of the story. That's when I decided to interview young moms to find out how they viewed the role of their own mother/mother-in-law as a grandparent. After listening to many stories, happy and not so happy, I realized how tough it can be on a young mom without the support and appreciation of her own mother/mother-in-law, which sadly is not always present. I discovered how prevalent this issue is which is why I began to interview these moms. I prefaced each interview with letting them know they had a choice as to whether or not they wanted to remain anonymous. I wanted them to feel comfortable giving the whole story rather than feeling like they had to tread lightly for fear of retribution if identified. I think the interviews were a real eye-opener, and I learned that while we are struggling for our grandparental rights, it is imperative that we acknowledge and appreciate how difficult motherhood can be and therefore be available to help out without offering unsolicited advice, which most likely would be misconstrued as criticism. I think this makes for a much healthier relationship and hopefully will lead to an ongoing dialogue. So, try sitting down together and listening to one another's wishes. Always begin on a positive note, giving honest compliments, and then gingerly express your feelings about the things that upset you. I know this may not work for everyone, but it can't hurt to give it a try. You may be pleasantly surprised, or, sadly, the boat will sink with you in it. But if you are prepared for the worst, you will be able to swim to shore unscathed.

Since the time I began writing this book, things have changed for me. While I set out to talk about how being a "grandma" is a state of mind, and that in this new century, what makes a grandma special isn't the same as when I was younger with my Grandma Rose and Grandma Fannie. It has truly taken me a long time to research, survey and write, and to get a general feel to what my fellow grandmothers deal with and how they see things. All the while staying true to my argument that I'm not the kind of grandmother who wears flower-print dresses and bakes cookies. I've said over and over again in this little yellow book that being a grandmother is a state of mind, and the state of my mind is that I'm still young, and viral, and full of energy, and my grandkids love me for it.

Maybe my days of playing tennis are over, but I can still run Hotel Nana and am proud to say, I have kept it a 5 Star Hotel. I may not be able to take my granddaughters to the mall for hours to try on outfit after outfit, but they understand when I say "I think it's time to go, we can come back another day." However, I can still carry on a lengthy conversation by texting and using the language of the times. These are things I pride myself on, and yes, we are all getting older and eventually, breaking down will happen, and how we deal with that is up to each of us individually. For me, I choose to keep a young attitude and to be the best grandparent I can be. And I hope that you do as well.

Oh, no, I think I am preaching again. I don't mean to, after all, we're in this together and sharing our thoughts is healthy and helpful. Maybe we should start a group called, "Grandmother's Anonymous" where it's safe to bitch and moan and bitch some more to one another (kindred spirits). I loved my Grandma Fannie and my Grandma Rose dearly, but as far as grandmothers go, we are eons apart and I love that we are.

Think about it; can you imagine your grandmother wearing tight jeans, working out or parasailing? I know I can't. We're a work in progress as far as keeping up with our grandkids. I wonder how our children will describe us when they become grandmothers? Remember, the only thing constant is change so keeping up with our grandkids isn't so easy. But I'm game; are you? Staying forever young is definitely a challenge, but one that I intend to take on. So what if I had to give up tennis and golf because of multiple back surgeries, and no longer can wear four-inch heels, or that I've definitely outgrown the miniskirts; as I've said, there's still plenty of ways to be a cool grandmother, rather than an old Granny. So, if you don't mind, please DON'T call me Grandma ... call me NANA!

# APPENDIX 1
# FUNNY STORIES
# AND MORE

I sent a survey to many of my "Grandmother friends" asking them to send me some true stories or exchanges they have had with their grandchildren. These are so funny that you might think they were made up; I promise that they are very true!

The following stories were sent to me by Eileen Orleans.

Stories:

Alex: (age 4) Mom, what does "core" mean?
Mom: Alex, give me an example.
Alex: Can't do that mom, but what does core mean?
Mom: Alex, if you give me an example I can help you.
Alex: Can't do that mom"
Mom: Alex, why can't you give me an example?
Alex: 'Cause mom, I don't know what example means.

*

My daughter was driving in her SUV and was quizzing her son, Alex, age 3, about what country he lives in, his phone number, address and asked, "what city do you live in?" From the way back her daughter, Rebecca, age 2, yells, "I know what city I live in!"

Surprised, my daughter asked, "What city do you live in Rebecca?"

"I live in Bagel City," she said, which is the place their father took them to every Sunday morning.

\*

Joe (age 5)
Me: Joe, do you know what you can give me for Hanukkah?
Joe: What?
Me: If you give me a hug and a kiss, I would be in Heaven.
Joe: Do you mean if I give you a hug and a kiss you'll be dead?

\*

Matt (age 9) upon hearing I was engaged:
Matt: Congratulations Nana!
Me: Anything you want me to tell Ronnie?
Matt: Yea, Congratulations GRANDPA!!

\*

Alex (age 2)
Alex: (Sitting on the toilet) "Mom I need the paper."

Mom comes running in with the toilet paper.
Alex: "Mom, not that paper, I need the sports page."

*

Rebecca (age 8)
Sitting with her grandfather and pretending to be a psychic:
"I see PopPop."
"I see PopPop with a hearing aid."

*

Joe: (age 6)
Alex, the oldest, had been teasing him
Mom: "Joe, just ignore him"
Joe: "Mom, that's a word that parents and teachers use – IT DOESN'T WORK!"

*

Matt: (age 7)
At his grandfather "Pops" funeral, the Priest was praising Edward; how he will be missed, his good deeds, etc. All is silent when Matt asks loudly, "Who in the heck is Edward"?

*

Joe: (age 6)
One afternoon I asked Joe to share his crackers with me and he said "no."

Later, after taking him to dinner, Joe asked me to buy some gum. I said "Joe, remember those cracker this afternoon – why should I share my gum?"
Joe (after thinking about it), "So Nana, is this the way you're going to be the rest of your life?"

\*

Matt: (age 7)
His oldest brother and sister are discussing a movie with their mother, telling her that she shouldn't see it due to the language and sexual content. From the other room Matt says: "It's fine for Mom, I've seen it twice."

\*

Rebecca: (age 16)
Me: "Rebecca, see my new engagement ring"
Rebecca: "One day that will be mine"
Me:" Rebecca, I'm not going anywhere"
Rebecca: "We'll see about that!"

Dylan, Rebecca, Nana (Eileen), Alex, Joe, Matt

***

**These stories are from Phyllis Feder.**

When Tyler was three and Jacob was four, they were playing in the kitchen and then decided to go and play outside. Since Jacob had no shoes on, his father, Todd, said, "Jacob, if you want to go outside, you need to put on your sandals." To which Jacob replied, "I don't want to wear those damn sandals!" And Todd said, "Jacob, I told you not to say that word!" And Tyler piped up with "Yeah, Jacob, don't say sandals!"

*

When we went to my father's unveiling, Hayley, 4, and Jessica, 3, were walking behind me toward the gravesite. Jessica was speaking in her normal (loud) voice and I overheard Hayley whisper to her, "Shh, Jessica, this is a very serious Jewish thing!" Since the rabbi did not show up, Sam (my husband) performed the service. A few months later, Hayley's dad lost one of his best friends and was preparing to go to the funeral. As he was leaving, Hayley said, "Daddy, if you are going to talk to God, then you should call Saba (my husband Sam) because he really knows how to talk to God."

*

Robin was trying to get Jessica to go to bed when she was about three. Robin tried reasoning with her and finally got annoyed with her. When Jessica heard this annoyed tone in Robin's voice, she sat down on the steps and said, "OK, mom, what's the deal?"

\*

One night when Jessica wanted Cocoa Puffs before dinner, Robin refused to give them to her. I happened to call at that moment and after she said "Hello," I heard Robin say to Jessica, "Do you want to tell Rag'm (that's me) why you are so angry?" To which Jessica replied, "I'm going to tell Rag'm to cancel your birthday!"

Jessica, Rag'm (Phyllis), Haley, Jacob, Tyler

\*\*\*

**These stories are from Sheilah Kaufman.**

Kaleb (my grandson) is two; we got him a swing and slide set with a little house. His dad put a carpet and a chair in the house and Kaleb's vacuum cleaner so he could keep it clean. When his mom gave him a warning not to do something where he could hurt himself, he told her, "You don't tell me NO either."

*

We took Kaleb to the zoo to see the wolves, hippo, pandas, lions, and elephants. The elephant pooped right in front of us. A few days later, Kaleb's mom looks out the window and sees Kaleb taking off his clothes and squatting on grass. When she yelled at him and asked him what he thought he was doing, he said, "Elephants poop in the grass, Kaleb poops in the grass!"

*

Kaleb broke his fake Croc shoes. When his mom took him to the mall for another pair, he stood up and yelled, "No fake Crocs! Real Crocs! Apparently the kids at day care teased him (we are talking about two-and-a-half to three-year-olds) because he did not have real $25 Crocs.

*

When Kaleb was going to Disney on his first airplane ride, his family got to the airport and Kaleb saw his first plane close up. After looking, and deciding he did not want to get on it, he told his father that he will get in their car, and his dad should drive and follow the plane to Florida!

*

While they were at Disney, I called to see how Kaleb was enjoying it. While my daughter and I discussed how expensive everything there is at Disney, Kaleb yells from the background, "Send Money!"

*

At age four, Kaleb told his mother, "You need to go to the hospital and get me a baby!"

*

After my mother died, Kaleb's other great-grandmother died. While visiting his grieving great-grandfather, my daughter told Kaleb to give his Poppa Jim an extra love because he is sad. Kaleb looked at him and said, "Why don't you go to the store and buy a new grown up to make you happy?"

*

Kaleb was five and had a girlfriend. While we were babysitting, he asked if he could call her. We didn't know he was not supposed to, so we dialed. The problem was, once he said, "Hi, what are you doing?" neither of them knew what to say. I guess the art of conversation comes later in life!

*

Kaleb heard lots of people telling his mother how great she looked during a party. Finally, he turned to her and asked, "What are you wearing?" His mom replied, "a shirt and a skirt." He thinks a minute then asks, "Can you wear it again tomorrow?"

*

We went to Sears to buy our daughter a new vacuum cleaner. Kaleb loves to clean at home, and was testing several models. On the way home, after our purchase, Kaleb asked his mom, "Can I have the house and the vacuum cleaner when you die, because they cost too much money!"

Caleb and Nana (Sheilah)

***

**These stories are from Sherry Sundick.**

When asked the question what other name would you pick for me other than Grandma Sherry, Reece Balamaci, age 4, said, "So smart" and Cameron Balamaci, age 7 said, "Wonderful."

*

When asked what makes a grandmother cool, Cameron said that when I'm watching him in school activities such as basketball and school performances. Reece said playing soccer is what makes grandmother cool. He said, "You are a little okay, but I am so much better." They also like to play hide and seek with me because I always hide in the same place. We also play a lot of catch together. It is a new experience playing with young boys as grandchildren since I raised two daughters. They are much more physical and sports oriented so I am not used to their high energy but I keep them busy by reading to them and doing puzzles and go to the movies with them.

*

When asked what a grandmother's job is, Cameron said, "A grandmother's job is to watch the grandkids." That is my biggest pleasure. Reece agreed and said, "I should keep my eyes open for people." We often have a lot of play dates at my daughter's house and I watch them play together.

Gavin, Grandma Sherry, Reece, Alexis, Cameron

\*\*\*

**I received this in an e-mail that was circulating, written by a teacher that asked her young students:**

WHAT IS A GRANDPARENT?

- Grandparents are a lady and a man who have no little children of their own. They like other people's.

- A grandfather is a man, and a grandmother is a lady!

- Grandparents don't have to do anything except be there when we come to see them.

- They are so old they shouldn't play hard or run.

- It is good if they drive us to the shops and give us money.

- When they take us for walks, they slow down past things like pretty leaves and caterpillars.

- They show us and talk to us about the colors of the flowers and also why we shouldn't step on "cracks."

- They don't say, "Hurry up."

- Usually grandmothers are fat, but not too fat to tie your shoes.

- They wear glasses and funny underwear.

- They can take their teeth and gums out.

- Grandparents don't have to be smart.

- They have to answer questions like "Why isn't God married?" and "How come dogs chase cats?"

- When they read to us, they don't skip. They don't mind if we ask for the same story over again.

- Everybody should try to have a grandmother, especially if you don't have television because they are the only grownups who like to spend time with us.

- They know we should have snack time before bedtime, and they say prayers with us and kiss us even when we've acted bad.

- My grandmother lives at the airport and when we want her, we just go get her. Then when we're done having her visit, we take her back to the airport.

- Grandpa is the smartest man on earth! He teaches me good things, but I don't get to see him enough to get as smart as him!

- It's funny when they bend over; you hear gas leaks, and they blame their dog.

# APPENDIX II
# GRANDMOTHERS
# AROUND THE WORLD

I asked for some stories from grandmothers from other cultures to better present the idea that we, as grandparents, are truly universal. Yes, I said it.

My Kid's Grandmothers
By Sara (last name withheld by request)

It is important to start by saying that my kids have a cultural mix in their grandparents.

My parents are 100 percent Honduran. My parents-in-law are Honduran, (father-in-law) and Colombian-American (mother-in-law). I feel my kids maternal grandparents (my parents) are actively involved in their upbringing and I would attribute this to two things: the relationship with a daughter (not a daughter-in-law), and the cultural background of Latin American families always including grandparents in daily family life and close relationship with grandkids.

My kid's relationship with my parents is not thought out, it is not planned, it is permitted without even noticing there should be a bit of permission, it is natural and desired, with sometimes spontaneous changes of plans and that is not a problem whatsoever. I believe this type of close relationship makes grandparents and grandchildren get to know each other in an ambiance that is natural.

My mother would leave her plans on hold to spend time with her grandkids. I honestly also think she sometimes does it to help her daughter out, and that is the only thing on her mind, to help.

My kids' relationship with their paternal grandparents is planned (most of the time), consulted, and there is a set time limit.

I am not trying to say there is more love in one home than the other; it's just that, to my perception, the level of comfort the children experience is different. My children are excited to visit both grandparents' houses always. The experience they share in each one is appreciated and different.

Sleepovers for the older ones (seven and eight-year-olds) are always fun in both houses. For the little ones, (four and one year-olds) it's easier accepted and they are willing to go to their maternal grandparent's house and spend the night.

In the beginning, I mentioned my mother-in-law is Colombian-American, her father was from Bogota, Colombia, and her mother is from Birmingham, Alabama. My mother-in-law is the fourth out of thirteen children! I had never met such a big family. The virtues and values I have learned from this family are absolutely incredible. The way independence and education of human will were, and are taught, are certainly things my husband teaches me daily towards the education we want for our kids.

So, when my kids spend time with their paternal grandparents, their experience is different and wonderful. They feel involved. They do not stop their activities to baby sit; they take the babies to their activities. It is quite an educational experience in itself.

My mother-in-law is a natural educator, and she was a preschool teacher for more than twenty years. So teaching them, especially hands on, and delegating tasks empowers them and boosts their self-esteem tremendously.

Having said that, even if meetings with their paternal grandparents are less often and planned and meetings with their maternal grandparents are more often and natural, they receive different manifestations of love and appreciation in different and unique ways that my children cherish and are making memories of. I feel delighted, extremely happy and blessed my children can enjoy two young and loving sets of grandparents and are actively involved in their lives today.

We don't know for how long we will have them, but I can sure remember my grandmother (the only one I knew), and those special moments with her. Grandparents and their teachings are irreplaceable and the joy they feel and express around their grandchildren is so beautiful to watch and be part of.

\*\*\*

## *My YiaYiah*
By Ava Carroll-Brown

As a first generation Greek, I am proud to say that I am now a *YiaYiah*, which of course is "Grandma" in Greek, and although I'm actually named after *my* YiaYiah, I am different in some ways yet exactly the same in others. Because of Greek tradition, I was the first-born daughter to the first-born son of the Doulgerakis family and was named after my father's mother: Evanthea. Because no one could pronounce my given name properly, my parents abbreviated it to "Ava" at a very early age; however the family responsibilities and expectations that came along with this name were instilled in my brain as a child and are practiced daily in *my* role as YiaYiah to seven wonderful grand munchkins.

Like so many cultures, in Greece, the women were taught to be subservient to the men. In fact in the vows of a Greek wedding ceremony, the words are repeated by the bride to her groom numerous times throughout this two-plus hour ritual and I quote: "*the woman will be subservient to the man; the maiden will be subservient to her master.*"

I remember as a little girl sharing meals with the family around my YiaYiah's dining table, and we, as "she creatures," as my brother thought of us, were not allowed to sit down until every male was seated and served, including my older brother. Wow, did he have fun with that rule. He would take his seat and then wait for me to take mine, and then he would pop up announcing that he needed something, like another fork or a second napkin. And you know what happened? My YiaYiah would look down the table directly at me and demand that I honor my brother's wishes and I would be forced to stand up and wait for him to be seated before I could sit back down. He took advantage of this tradition to torment me.

My YiaYiah was a very strong woman, respected by the community, and of course her family. She was always in charge of any community effort to help a family in need by knocking on the doors of neighbors and gathering food, clothing and anything else that may be needed in a time of loss or sorrow. She was always available to comfort and console her friends and family with an embrace or a funny story. I watched her for years and as I grew working hard to follow in her footsteps with kindness and understanding, I knew in my heart that there was a lot more to this strong name that I was given, there was responsibility and that was all right by me.

But for every similarity that we share, my YiaYiah and I, we also have our differences. After all, times have changed.

I work hard to teach the lessons of community responsibility and strong patriotic beliefs, as well as actions, and I can see my YiaYiah standing proud in every step I take. I try to keep a few of the Greek words flowing in our household but no one is fluent in the language, including me. I always tell people that I understand Greek better than I speak it, especially when I am being reprimanded or scolded in Greek. Some words you never forget.

My YiaYiah never wore a stitch of makeup and her long gray hair was always pinned up in a braid bun. I would never walk out the door without my hair blown straight and perfect makeup.

The thing that I remember the most was my YiaYiah always told us to be true to ourselves; which was her way of saying never tell a lie with the added threat that my nose would grow if I did. So when I was afraid to tell my parents the real story, I would sit in the bathroom sink, look in the mirror and lie to see if my nose really did grow and you know what? I would imagine that it did; hence, the honestly is the best policy phrase holds true to my heart.

This wonderful lady with the strength of an army, yet the warmth of the morning sun and an occasional white hair growing from her chin, which I would pull every time I saw her was truly the matriarch of our family and as the first granddaughter born to the family, she felt strongly that when the time came, I should fill her shoes; which has not been an easy task.

For an old world Greek woman from another country, my YiaYiah was truly ahead of her time. Even though she has been gone for almost 30 years, there is not a day that goes by that I am not reminded of her lessons and her strengths and the pride I feel that I am now YiaYiah to my grandkids. Only one of my granddaughters will carry the family name of Evanthea or Ava as the case may be – she is now 4-years-old and I see her strength and am confident that the traditions of my YiaYiah will be in the family through this strong, smart little girl for years to come.

***

Here is a short list of names for grandmothers in other countries around the world. It is not comprehensive, but gives you an idea. I found this fascinating, and I hope you do too.

> *HAWAII – Tutu*
> *SCOTLAND – Granny or Nanna*
> *SWEDEN – Mormor*
> *GREECE -- YiaYiah*
> *JAPAN – O-baa-san or Baa-baa*
> *FRANCE – Mamie or Memee*
> *IRELAND – Nana (I guess I must be Irish!)*
> *YIDDISH – Bubbie or Bubby*
> *HUNGARY – Nagyi or Nagymami*
> *POLAND – Babka*
> *CANTONESE – MaMa*
> *INDONESIA – Nanek*
> *UKRAIN – Baba*
> *PHILIPPINES – Lola*
> *RUSSIA – Babaor or Babushka*
> *SPANISH – Abuela*
> *GERMAN – Oma*
> *PORTUGUESE – Vova*
> *ARABIC – Jedda*
> *VIET NAM – Ba*

***

I am sure there are variations depending on whom you talk to, but I found it so interesting that we use many of the above names; I am Nana and some friends are Mimi, or Memee or other variations of the spelling. I often referred to my grandmother as Granny, but never called her that to her face. I felt it was not respectful but I do like the sound of it.

I also learned a lot from **www.AboutGrandparents. com** that I will share with you briefly.

Grandparents are vital in African-American families as well as in Hispanic families. They typically have considerable authority, especially in extended large families. Many grandparents are the ones raising their grandchildren, and many more also live in the same house. A Vietnamese friend of mine told me that her married children and their children live with her. Grandparents are very important in her culture and often make important decisions. She said that living here in our country has "Americanized" their culture but when she returns to Vietnam to be with her family, it is a different story. She had better listen to her mother and grandmother or she is in big trouble. They treat her like a child because she had better not disobey them. Can you imagine someone trying to control your every move?

No way, Jose! We are so liberated that we can't imagine any other way of life; I love my life just the way it is so if I want to "kick ass" because I am disrespected, then you bet your bootie I will! I know all you grandma's out there are shaking your heads in agreement.

My Grandma Fannie was always in the Kitchen

My Grandma Rose celebrating her 90th birthday

Scott, Camryn, Jaclyn, Cole and Lisa

Nana and Grandpa clowning around for Halloween

Breakfast in bed at NANA's HOTEL
Jaclyn, Camryn and Cole

Isaac, Bonnie, Todd and Brian

Me and my "Grandma Sisters"
Nana (Me), Grammy (Arlie), Rag'm (Phyllis),
Nana (Sydney), below Nana (Barbara)

They keep me smiling!
Norm, Brian, Shawn, Bonnie, Me, Lisa and Scott

Meme (Francine), Lily, Evan and Alexandra.

Darian, Justin, Mimi(Ellen), Layla, Jillian and Tyler

# APPENDIX III
# OTHER NAMES FOR
# GRANDMOTHER

After researching alternative names for "Grandma," it seems that most grandmothers have had a name in mind even before their grandchild was born. Then their little one learns to make sounds and happens to repeat the same sound whenever you appear. If he/she reaches for you while making the sound, guess who just might decide on what to call you?

As I said earlier, the name "Grandma" has been replaced by all of the names listed below by a doting grandmother just like you. And this list is also not comprehensive. New names are added daily, but this will give you an idea of the variety of names for grandmothers all around the world.

| | | |
|---|---|---|
| Abuelita | Azuela | Bam Bam |
| Ama | Ba | Bebe |
| Amie | Baba | Bee Ma |
| Angel | Bama | Bela |

| | | |
|---|---|---|
| Big Momma | Gram | Jan Jan |
| Bon Bon | Grambo | Jiggy G |
| Boppie | Gram Gram | Ju Ju |
| Bube | Grammie | La La |
| Bubbie | Grammy | Lalita |
| Bushka | Grammy Bear | Le Le |
| Cita (Mama | Grammy Toots | Lita |
| Cita) | Grams | Lola |
| Darling Dear | Gramsie | Lolly (pairs |
| Dee | Gran | with Pop) |
| Dee Dee | Grancie | Lovie |
| Diva | Gran Cookie | Madam |
| Doe Doe | Grandma | Madonna |
| Doodles | Grandmama | Mame |
| Drammaw | Grand Mauu | Mamere |
| Drammie | Grandnana | Mamie |
| Flower | Grandmom | Marmie |
| Gaga | Grandmommy | Mayma |
| Gam | Grandmother | Memee |
| Gammaw | Grannie | Mim |
| Gamie | Groovy | Mima |
| Sunshine | Grammy | Mimi |
| Gamma Mie | Groovy Grams | Min |
| Gammy | Honey | Minnie |
| Gamz | Honey Bea | Mom |
| Gee Gee | Honey Bear | Mom Mom |
| Gigi | Hunny | Momo |
| Glama | Ice Cream | Mooma |
| Go Go | Grandma | Moppy |
| Goo Goo | Izzie | Mum Mum |

My Mom

Nan

Nana

Nana-Banana

Nana (add

name)

Nana-Pie

Nannie

Nanny

Neenie

Nini

Nona

Nonie

Nonna

Nutty Nana

Oma

Oomie

Peaches

Precious

Queenie

Ragu'm

Ramaw

Sa Sa

Sassy

Sugar

Sweetie

Sweet Honey

Tiger

Tita

Toots

Tootsie

Tutti

Tutu

Va Va

Ya Ya

Yiahyah

Zaide

Zsa Zsa

CPSIA information can be obtained at www.ICGtesting.com
Printed in the USA
BVOW08*2037111215

429352BV00003B/4/P